The Power of Numbers

Why Europe needs to
get younger

GW00686391

Richard Ehrman

June 2009

Policy
Exchange

UBP
University of Buckingham Press

First published 2009 by Policy Exchange
and The University of Buckingham Press Ltd

Policy Exchange
Clutha House
10 Storey's Gate
London SW1P 3AY

www.policyexchange.org.uk

Distributed by
The University of Buckingham Press
Buckingham MK18 1EG
+44 1280 828338

www.ubpl.co.uk

ISBN 978-1-906097-06-6

Designed by SoapBox, www.soapboxcomunications.co.uk

Contents

Foreword   1
Executive Summary   3
Introduction   12

1   Some History   23
   Sages Through the Ages   31

2   The Intricacies of Demography   38
   Demographic Transition   39
   Living for Ever   40
   Fertility and Population Momentum   42
   Can We Trust the Projections?   45

3   What is going to happen?   50
   Asia   51
   The Americas   52
   Africa and the Middle East   53
   Europe   54
   Britain   57

4   The Consequences   63
   Population Pyramid Selling   65
   The Clash of Generations   70
   The Power of Numbers   75
   The Military Equation   79
   The Human Stain   82

5   Can we do anything about it?   88
   Immigration   90
   Work Till You Drop   100
   The Baby Famine   108

Conclusion   125
Appendix   135

Foreword

To an extent that most of us have yet to grasp, demographic change is going to affect us all in the coming decades. The aim of this short book is to provide a layman's guide to what's happening to our population, and consider what, if anything, we might do to influence it.

My background is that of a journalist, not a demographer, and in writing it I have been helped by a variety of people and institutions. As well as the teams at both Policy Exchange and the University of Buckingham Press, I would like, in particular, to thank Simon Horner who did the research for the book and without whose patience and untiring efforts it would never have been written. I would also like to thank David Coleman, Professor of Demography at Oxford University, who read the book in draft and offered many valuable insights, suggestions and corrections. Finally I am most grateful to Philip Mould, who provided generous financial support for the project.

Richard Ehrman. June 2009

Executive Summary

Britain and Europe are likely to emerge from the credit crunch only to find that they are at the beginning of a long demographic crunch. Over the next fifty years Japan, Russia and many European countries face a sustained, outright fall in population - something that has never happened before in any advanced economy. For most other European nations the prospect is one of ageing stagnation and high immigration.

Politicians and policymakers were already worried about the effect of an ageing population on future economic growth, even before the financial crisis struck. By the middle of the next decade the shrinking ratio of working-age people to pensioners will start to exert a downward drag on growth. By 2050 countries in Western Europe will go from having roughly four people of working age supporting every pensioner to just two.

Political leaders recognise the problems that this will cause for pensions and healthcare, but there has been surprisingly little discussion of the wider demographic dilemma that now confronts us. Demography affects, and is affected by, a lot more than pensions and social security; immigration, the way the labour market functions, the availability of housing and training, tax and social security all play an important part in shaping the structure and composition of the population. But, on the subject of population, politicians and policy makers have been surprisingly slow to join up the dots.

An Unbalanced Population: The demographic crunch has its origins in the 1970s when, following the postwar baby boom, fertility fell dramatically right across non-communist Western Europe. This is the main reason that that we now face the prospect of a rapidly rising number of older people, and a relative shortage of younger, working age people to support them. The big problem with the British population is not that it is too large (although many think it is) or too small, but that it has become unbalanced.

So far, we have been able to take a relaxed view of our worsening demography only because the biggest economic challenge of all, the retirement of the baby boomers, is still ahead of us. Even this, however, is no longer far away. From 2010 onwards, those born immediately after the Second World War will start reaching 65. By 2015 – barely five years away – the peak post-war cohort born in the '50s and early '60s will start retiring. It is only when this happens that the full economic impact of our declining demography will start to be felt.

Immigration: Politicians' plans to balance the demographic books over the coming decades have tended to rely heavily on the assumption that there will continue to be very high net immigration. For Britain the assumption is that net immigration – that is, the balance between immigrants and emigrants – will average 190,000 a year for the foreseeable future, or nearly two million a decade. But is it credible that voters will accept this? Over recent years, it has become apparent that immigration can sometimes cause as many problems as it solves. A YouGov poll in November 2007 found that over 81% of voters wanted the Government to "substantially reduce" immigration levels.[1]

It would certainly make a huge difference to the outlook for our population if the official assumption on immigration were altered. According to the UK Government, the population will increase from 61 million people today to 75 million people by 2050. Without immigration it would rise to just 64 million by 2031, mainly because of people living longer, before starting to decline. This is a pretty big difference.

Finding More Workers From Among Our Own Ranks: If we are not going to rely so heavily on immigration then we will have to find more workers from among our own ranks. No one doubts that there is plenty of scope to improve Europe's chronically inefficient labour markets. But for governments, including Britain's, it has often been easier to fall back on the quick fix of immigration than to tackle such deep-seated problems as benefit reform and inadequate training. In many countries, it is striking how high unemployment coexists with high immigration.

1 YouGov poll on behalf of Migration Watch; http://www.migrationwatchuk.com/pdfs/other/10_18_re-sultsformw_immigrationomi2908_nov_07.pdf

Changing this, however, will not be simple. To quote the former European Commissioner, Frits Bolkestein: "Pay more, work longer and get less, is not an easy message to sell." But if we are to overcome the huge economic hurdle posed by the retirement of the baby boomers, without resort to further mass immigration, then Europe's governments will have to get to grips not just with pensions and retirement ages, but with their labour markets generally. With the retirement of the baby boomers almost upon us, they have already left it desperately late.

The Birth Rate: When we think about how fast society is ageing, we usually attribute it to the fact that we are living longer. But while this is so, it is important to realise that increased longevity is not the only reason that the average age is rising. In fact, it is half the story at most. Just as significant is that, across Europe, there are fewer young people to reduce the average (and support their elders). Ageing is as much about this as it is about increased life expectancy.

In the longer term, if Europe is to have any hope of addressing its demographic problems it needs to get younger. But how? If a more balanced population is not going to be brought about by high levels of net immigration, then European countries will need to encourage higher fertility.

As far as the UK is concerned, as well as more people arriving in the country, net immigration has a secondary effect on the growth of the

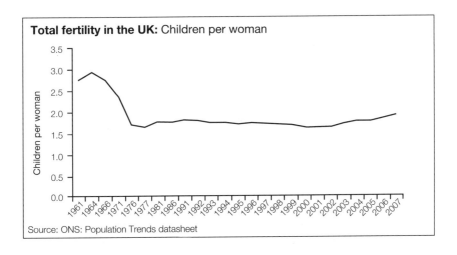

Total fertility in the UK: Children per woman

Source: ONS: Population Trends datasheet

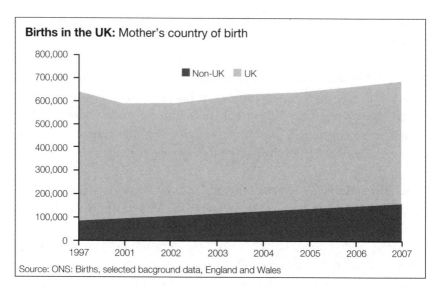

Births in the UK: Mother's country of birth

Source: ONS: Births, selected bacground data, England and Wales

population. Recent migrants have a higher level of fertility than those born in the UK – approximately two-and-a-half children for every woman compared to one-and-three-quarters for those born in the UK.[2] This has helped to drive the birth rate up recently, but the number of children born to the average woman is still below the "replacement rate" of about 2.1 which would lead to a shrinking population without further immigration.

Yet surveys carried out by the OECD show that in almost all developed countries people would like to have more children than they actually do. For example in the UK women on average say that they would like 2.5 children, whereas they are having less than two (see page 112-3). If there is widespread "baby hunger" then what is it that is stopping people from having more children?

What determines how many children people have? Several factors seem to have a clear impact on fertility, and tackling these issues could help to close the gap between how many children people want and how many they have:

2 News release, Office for National Statistics, December 2007; http://www.statistics.gov.uk/pdfdir/fertility1207.pdf

- *Youth unemployment.* In a 1999 study the three EU countries with the worst youth unemployment also had the lowest fertility. The unemployment rate in 2006 for women aged 15-24 in Italy was 27%, in Greece it was 29 per cent. Where people cannot support themselves financially they are likely to delay having children.

- *Flexibility* – women's chances to combine motherhood with a job. This in turn reflects the flexibility of the labour market. As well as reducing youth unemployment, a flexible labour market makes it easier for women to leave and re-enter work: Europe's more flexible economies are more likely to offer part-time jobs and also temporary work which can fit in around school holidays. The wider spread of flexible working arrangements and job splits, flexible hours, and home working are also likely to boost women's ability to combine motherhood and a job.

- *Childcare and benefits.* A reasonably high level of financial support from the state in the form of maternity leave, child support, day care etc. As the OECD chart below shows, low-fertility Italy, Spain and Greece are among the lowest spenders on childcare. Conversely France, Sweden and the UK all spend more than average on them.

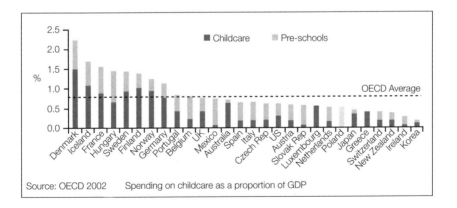

Source: OECD 2002   Spending on childcare as a proportion of GDP

- *Attitudes to marriage and illegitimacy*. In Europe very low fertility countries tend to be socially conservative, and their level of births out of wedlock has risen far more slowly than in other advanced countries, as the graph from the OECD below shows.

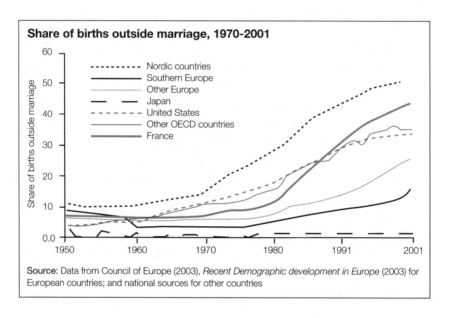

Share of births outside marriage, 1970-2001

Source: Data from Council of Europe (2003), *Recent Demographic development in Europe* (2003) for European countries; and national sources for other countries

- *Housing is crucial*. Countries where young people move out of their family home later have lower fertility. A study in 2001 found that in Denmark, half of all young men have left home before they are 22, while in Italy it is not until almost age 30 that half of all men have left home. The equivalent ages for women were 20 in Denmark and 27 in Italy.[3]

In Britain, we score well on the availability of part-time work and the flexibility of the labour market. But, over the last decade, taxes and other charges that hit the young disproportionately, like student debt, stamp duty, petrol duty and council tax, have all risen sharply. So has the cost of housing, even after the recent downturn.

3 Iacovou M, "Leaving Home in the European Union", Working Papers for the Institute of Social and Economic Research, No 18,University of Essex, November 2001

The International Context: Just as in Britain, fertility began to fall in the 1970s right across the non-communist developed world. After the collapse of communism, the same happened in the former Soviet Union and Eastern Europe in the 1990s. Since then birth rates have recovered in most of Northern and Western Europe, although not to the level at which the population will replace itself. But in the countries of Southern, Central, and Eastern Europe fertility remains obstinately stuck at levels that are alarmingly low.

As a result, many of these countries face a sustained, outright fall in population between now and 2050. This split will have important consequences for the balance of power and influence in Europe. It also has the potential to create powerful tensions within the EU as the "population vacuum" on Europe's periphery sucks in people from the fast-growing countries of North Africa and the Near East.

Meanwhile, in most of the rest of the world numbers will continue to grow strongly. This shifting of the demographic plates will lead to huge political, economic and cultural changes, which people are only just beginning to think about. In Asia the economic dominance of Japan, which faces the same sort of demographic problems as the worst affected European countries, looks set to be eclipsed, first by China then by India. In the Middle East and Africa, rapid population growth is more likely to fuel instability than prosperity. In Europe, the risk is the opposite, that ageing and falling populations will further undermine both the continent's social model and its economy.

Recommendations

1) We should abandon the assumption that mass immigration is the way to balance the demographic books. Even the Government now seems to realise that letting immigration continue at its current rate could cause as many problems as it solves.

2) Britain should draw up a population strategy: No government should go anywhere near telling people what size of family they should be aiming for. But that does not mean we should have no opinion on what size of population we want and how we might influence it. At the very least, we need a strategy to deal with the demographic challenges we are going to be facing over the next few decades. Scotland now has an explicit population target and the UK Government should consider adopting one too. If we could achieve a stable and balanced population, the advantages not just for the economy, but also for the environment, for the sustainability of welfare, health and other social systems, and for fairness between the generations, would be considerable.

3) A Royal Commission on Population: Many things that the Government does affect the growth of population; from the tax and benefits system to labour market regulation and housing policy. In 1946 the Government set up a Royal Commission on Population. Its 270-page report, published in 1949, provides a model for a comprehensive review of population policy. It linked up everything from welfare to town planning to the implications of demographics for foreign policy. A similar exercise would be valuable 60 years on.

4) Raise the retirement age faster and increase labour market participation: The retirement age should be raised more quickly. In Britain, the pension age for women is set to rise from 60-65 between 2010 and 2020, and then to 68 for both sexes in 2048. In the US – despite its comparatively favourable demographics – the pension age for everybody is meant to rise to 67 by 2027. The UK and other European countries should aim to match this at the very least. At the same time European countries need to embrace radical labour market and welfare reforms to raise the employment rate.

5) Redouble efforts to educate the public about the costs of ageing: The challenge posed to the public finances by the demographic crunch will, if anything, be even greater than the difficulties we now face as a result of the credit crunch. But politicians across Europe have found it difficult to take action to address the consequences of their ageing societies. In Britain, the Government does produce regular fiscal sustainability reports drawing together information on the cost of our changing demography. However, they rarely receive much publicity and many of the assumptions on which they are based are too optimistic. The Government needs to make them more rigorous, and give them more prominence.

6) Prepare for the global consequences of a shifting and growing world population: One hundred years ago, a quarter of the world's population was European, now the figure is just 11 % and this relative decline is set to continue. It is not so much that Europe has been shrinking – at least not yet – but that others have been growing faster. Europeans should prepare for a changed balance of power in the world. Such preparation should cover a wide range of questions – for example: Europe's ability to project power and wage war in future; the coming struggles over resources (particularly energy); and investment in agricultural research, which will be necessary if the world is to feed a global population that's set to get not just larger but also more prosperous.

Politicians often talk about the need for joined up government, and demography is an area that needs it more than most. Yet the subject of population change still gets far less attention in this country than climate change, even though we can be just as sure that it will transform the way we live – and probably in ways that are easier to predict.

Introduction

If demography really is destiny, then Britain should be feeling pretty smug. In the summer of 2008 the number of people in the UK passed the 61 million mark, an increase of a million in just two years. By 2031, according to the latest government projections, there will be over 70 million of us, and perhaps 75 million by 2050.[4] By European standards, this makes us exceptional. While our numbers are booming, across much of the rest of the continent populations are stagnating, and some are even shrinking. So why does this bountiful prospect make so many of us uneasy? A century ago it would probably have been greeted with jubilation as another sign of national virility and self-confidence, but not today. And can it really be true?

On the latest projections from both the European Commission and the United Nations, Britain is set to become the largest member of the EU by 2050, overtaking Germany which today has a population nearly 20 million greater than ours.[5] Yet we are also told that we are ageing as a society at a rate that many experts feared, even before the sudden onset of the credit crunch, would bankrupt our pensions and health systems. If we really do overtake Germany it will not be down to a baby boom, but because of the high recent rate of immigration. In August 2008, just as Brussels said that we are on course to become the most numerous country in Europe, Britain's own Office of National Statistics announced that, for the first time since records began, we have more pensioners than children.[6] No wonder that we are confused and alarmed by what is happening to our population.

4 National Projections, Office for National Statistics, 2006; http://www.statistics.gov.uk/CCI/nugget.asp?ID=1352&Pos=1&ColRank=2&Rank=864

5 Population Projections, Eurostat, 9th January 2009; http://epp.eurostat.ec.europa.eu/tgm/table.do?tab=table&init=1&plugin=1&language=en&pcode=tps00002

6 News release, Office for National Statistics, 21st August 2008; http://www.statistics.gov.uk/cci/nugget.asp?ID=949

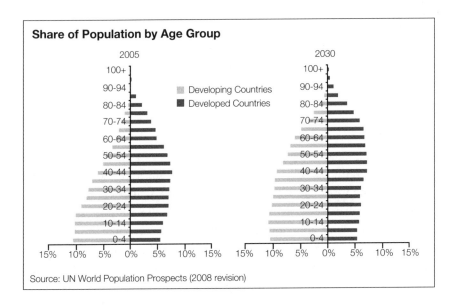

Share of Population by Age Group

2005   2030

Developing Countries
Developed Countries

Source: UN World Population Prospects (2008 revision)

A global shift of power

Nor are we the only ones. Around the globe most countries are facing demographic upheaval, many on a scale far greater than we are. During the last 50 years populations increased pretty much across the board in developed and undeveloped countries alike, albeit at different rates. Today the demographic plates are not just shifting, but diverging. Between now and 2050 a number of European countries face a sustained outright fall in population – something that has never happened before in any advanced economy. For most of the rest of Europe, the prospect is one of ageing stagnation, even after substantial immigration is taken into account.

In stark contrast, across much of the rest of the world numbers will continue to grow strongly. Eventually, perhaps in the second half of this century, population growth in the developing world, too, will moderate. Before that happens, however, demographic divergence between today's developed and developing worlds will revolutionise the balance of political and economic power between regions and countries.

According to the United Nations, the world's population is increasing by nearly 80 million a year, or one and a half million people a week, and by 2010 is expected to stand at just over 6.9 billion overall. Of these, approximately

1.2 billion will live in the developed world and 5.7 billion in the developing world. By 2050 the UN expects the world's population to have grown to 9.1 billion people, with nearly all the increase accounted for by the developing world. Populations are also set to get a lot older worldwide, with the proportion of over 65s projected to more than double from 7 to 16% between 2005–50. In the developed world the equivalent increase will be from 15 to 26%.

Projecting current trends into the future is always hazardous but, barring anything cataclysmic, it seems reasonable to assume that in half a century's time the world's population will be significantly older and 30% larger, and the vast majority of these extra people will be Asians, Africans, Arabs and Latin Americans. Very few of them will be European.

Nor are we talking about the distant future here, many of these changes are already underway. Britain, together with its near neighbours France and Ireland, is still growing and projected to go on doing so. In the rest of North and Western Europe the outlook is for populations that will age, but remain fairly static overall. Elsewhere, however, the story is very different. Parts of Europe have been depopulating for over two decades. In Central, Southern and Eastern Europe fertility fell below replacement level as long ago as the '70s. In the '80s and '90s it fell even further in many places to what demographers term lowest-low fertility – a birth rate of just 1.3 children per woman or even less.

To get a better feel for what this will mean one has to look at the population projections for individual countries, some of which are truly amazing. Between 2005 and 2050 Russia is expected to lose 27 million people, which is nearly 20% of its current total. To put it even more starkly, Russia is losing 10,000 people a week, and is expected to go on doing so for the next 40 years. In the other European countries of the former Soviet Union, the outlook is, if anything, even bleaker: in both Ukraine and Belarus the decline is expected to be nearer 25%.

Moving west, Poland had a population of 38 million in 2005; by 2050 the demographers at the UN expect that to have fallen to under 32 million. Over the same period they expect Bulgaria to lose 30% of its population, Latvia, Lithuania and Romania 20% each, Croatia 15% and Hungary 10%. In what Donald Rumsfeld dismissively termed "old" Europe, the number of Germans is set to fall 15%, or 12 million, by 2050. Were it not for massive immigration the number of Italians and Spaniards would be set for even larger falls.

Meanwhile, as populations in Europe age, stagnate and shrink, in most of the rest of the world they will be getting larger, and often much larger. So as well as confronting its own demographic decline, the continent will also have to grapple with the implications of dramatic population change beyond its borders. The US is projected to grow from 300 million today to 400 million by mid-century, and its average age will also rise by far less than Europe's. But it is in the developing world that numbers will really soar.

To take just a few examples: the Indian population is expected to increase by 55 % between 2005-2050, taking it to more than 1,600 million and overtaking China. In the Middle East, Iraq is expected to double from 30 million now to more than 60 million over the same period, while Saudi Arabia is projected to increase from 24 to 44 million, and Iran by 40% from 70 to just under 100 million. On the southern shores of the Mediterranean, Egypt is expecting its population to rise by 70% between 2005 and mid-century, or more than 50 million extra people. In Sub-Saharan Africa the projected increases are even more startling. Between 2010 and 2020 – in just a single decade – the UN expects the population of this region to soar by over 200 million.[7]

The End of an Economic Bonanza

A falling population need not necessarily be bad, indeed as far as protecting the environment and reducing pollution are concerned it could well be beneficial. But in industrial societies, at least in peacetime, rising populations have usually been able to generate enough economic growth not just to maintain their standard of living, but to improve it. Like it or not, modern life, and especially modern social security and pension systems, are predicated on growth. For all those countries now faced with the prospect of a significantly smaller or older population within just a few decades, the big question is how are they going to get from here to there without massive economic and social dislocation?

In Europe a demographic golden age is drawing to a close. For at least the last 200 years, the power of numbers has been on our side. Europe's expansion around the globe was based on buoyant population, just as much as it was on military might and technological supremacy. Even in the 20th century, when the continent was ravaged by two huge wars, its population still continued to

7 For an explanation of how the UN compiles its population projections and why they will be the main ones used in this book, see page 38

grow. For the last 50 years we have enjoyed an economic bonanza based not just on peace and technological progress, but also on remarkably favourable demographics. The credit crunch notwithstanding, those of us who were born in the postwar baby boom of the '50s and '60s know that we have been a lucky generation. Not only have we never had to go to war, but the welfare state, the consumer society, huge technological and medical advances, cheap travel and food, and many other advantages, have given us an easier, more prosperous life than all but the richest of our forebears could even dream of.

Best of all in economic terms, has been that we are baby boomers. In 1964, at the peak of the boom, just over a million babies were born in Britain; 40 or so years later, in 2007 the figure was 690,013 – and that came after several years when the birth rate fell below 600,000.[8] For a parent having a baby today, let alone for a newborn child, the difference between being one-in-a-million and one-in seven-hundred-thousand has no immediate personal impact. But for those fortunate enough to be born in the '50s and '60s being one of so many has been an enormous economic bonus – at least so far.

Thanks to the baby boom, the number of young people coming into the job market across both Europe and North America in the 1970s and 1980s comfortably outnumbered those who were then reaching pension age. Demographers call such favourable periods a "demographic window". Now this is about to go into reverse, savagely so in some countries. Soon our demographic window will close and there will be fewer people working to support an increasing number of pensioners.

And to make matters worse – in dry economic terms – not only will there be more pensioners but they will live much longer. There are, of course, many good things about living longer, not least that on a personal level it is what we all wish for. But between 2011 – just two years away – and 2050 the European Commission's statistical office, Eurostat, expects that the number of those of working age will have declined by over 50 million, while the numbers of those of pensionable age will have more than doubled.[9]

8 Live Birth Statistics, Office for National Statistics, December 2008; http://www.statistics.gov.uk/cci/nugget.asp?id=369
9 Population Projections, Eurostat press release, April 2005

Europe's baby bust

The main reason for this sudden reversal of momentum in Europe's popula-tion is the drop in fertility that began in the 1970s, when in many countries the baby boom turned abruptly into a baby bust. To calculate a country's fertility, demographers use a measure called the total fertility rate (TFR), which is defined as the number of children a woman can expect to have in her lifetime. For a country to reproduce itself, it needs a TFR of 2.1 children per woman. The average for all 27 countries of the EU is currently 1.5 and across large swathes of the continent it is even lower.

With overall numbers due to begin falling in just a few years time and populations starting to age rapidly, the demographic predicament facing many European countries is about to become acute, even dangerous. In those which are most exposed, people are just beginning to realise that the seismic demographic shifts about to unfold will pose a threat not just to their standard of living, but to their whole way of life. Addressing a convention of Euro-pean bishops in Rome in March 2007, Pope Benedict was blunt about the danger ahead: "From a demographic point of view", warned His Holiness, "one must note that Europe seems to be following a path that could lead to its departure from history. This not only places economic growth at risk; it could also create enormous difficulties for social cohesion…One could almost think that the European continent is in fact losing faith in its own future."

As a German living in Italy, it is perhaps not surprising that the Pope views the continent's demography with such foreboding. But before we all get too gloomy it is important to emphasise that the picture across Europe is far from uniform.

Over recent years a marked gap has opened up between North and West Europe, where fertility is typically between 1.7 and 2 children per woman, and the South, Centre and East where no country has a TFR above 1.5 (with the lone exception of Estonia). In effect, there is a European fertil-ity line that now divides the continent, almost as the Berlin Wall used to divide it politically. For those to the North and West of it the demographic outlook, while hardly rosy, is a lot better than it is elsewhere.

Furthermore, a country's TFR is not the only thing that determines its demographic outlook. Up to now, the impact of low fertility has gener-ally been masked by the old living longer and by immigration. Together with fertility, both of these factors will play a crucial part in deciding how Europe's demography will pan out over the coming decades.

Longevity has risen substantially over the last 20 years across Western Europe, and also most of Eastern Europe. The big exception to this has been among the countries which used to be part of the old Soviet Union. In some of these, notably Russia, life expectancy has actually fallen since communism collapsed. But, as far as the EU is concerned, rising longevity is something all its members, even those that were once part of the USSR, now have in common. By contrast, migration, both within Europe and from outside, has been much more varied. With the exception of Poland, all the big countries of the EU (those with populations of 30 million or more) have attracted large-scale immigration over the last 20 years, as have many of the medium-sized and small states. However, among the large ones Italy, Spain and Britain have taken far more than Germany and France, while most of Eastern Europe is still a zone of emigration.

What will really determine which European countries grow, which stagnate and which shrink between now and mid-century is the extent to which fertility and migration balance each other out (or fail to). It is because Germany combines low fertility with comparatively low immigration that it is projected to shrink. And it is because Spain, whose fertility is only marginally higher, has recently been taking up to five times as many immigrants as Germany despite having just half the population, that it is projected to grow strongly over the next 25 years.

For Britain, which combines reasonably high fertility with distinctly high immigration, such a calculation could be thought reassuring – at least at first glance. It is certainly the reason that we are now projected to grow faster than any other major country in Europe. But even those countries that are expected to keep on growing will not escape the fallout if a large part of the EU runs into severe demographic difficulties; we may not feel the full impact, but we will surely feel some of it.

It would also be wrong to think that while other European countries will be grappling with demographic decline, in Britain our problems will be all about expansion. If one looks behind the headlines, it soon becomes apparent that our longer term demographic trends, while certainly more robust than in most of Europe, are not as different as we might think.

Immigration may help to boost overall numbers and even to keep them steady or growing when they would otherwise be falling. But it is not the demographic panacea that is sometimes portrayed.

As we will see later, even if immigration were to continue at its recent high level, it still would not be enough to offset the huge rise in the number of pensioners that is about to hit all European countries. In Britain's case the upsurge in immigration has also been relatively sudden and it is very likely that it could decline again, perhaps sooner than we reckon. A significant number of East Europeans may return home as the economy in this country turns down, or the number of new arrivals may simply be curbed by political fiat. If immigration does fall, the trajectory of the British population would look much more prosaic, with numbers increasing modestly due to longevity over the next 20 years, before starting gently to decline.

Do We Need a Population Strategy?

Drive around the M25 at rush hour and you can see why people might welcome such an outcome. If the population were to increase by nine million over the next 20 or so years as a result of immigration it would not be quite 'standing room only'. But in South East England, in particular, it could feel uncomfortably like it. The pressure on housing and public services would be enormous, perhaps even unsustainable. It could also have huge repercussions for race relations and social cohesion generally.

Even the Government now seems to realise that letting immigration continue at its current rate could cause a crisis. But reducing immigration will not be problem-free either. Large parts of the economy have come to depend on migrant labour. Cut back on it too sharply or suddenly, even in difficult times like today's, and we risk serious economic damage.

Britain does not have (and has never had) an official population policy, and the question is sometimes asked whether we need one. The problem with trying to frame such a policy is that demography is complicated; it both affects and is affected by a wide array of things that people often do not associate it with. Nor should the Government go anywhere near telling people what size of family they should be aiming for. On the other hand, a huge amount of what the Government does will have an effect on the growth or decline of the population: not just immigration but also housing and planning law, labour market rules, the tax and benefits system, and the provision of childcare. As we grapple with these, it would be helpful if we had some sense of what size of population we want.

In economic terms, growing populations have generally been advantageous. On environmental grounds, there is an obvious case for trying to shrink our numbers. As far as social cohesion and fairness between the generations are concerned, there is a lot to be said for a stable population. Which should we be aiming for? It is a question we need to answer, and to do so we need a far greater awareness of how important population is to a whole range of issues that we do not necessarily connect it with, and also of how many different factors can have an impact on our demography.

First, and most widely understood, are the financial problems associated with an ageing society. For decades now, the finances of most European governments have been based on what might be termed population pyramid selling. The European social model of universal, publicly-funded benefits has always depended on a plentiful supply of tax. But it was only in the '60s and '70s, as the baby boomers entered the labour market, that governments were able to increase their tax take and the notion of big government really took off. The question policymakers should be asking themselves now is not just how to pay for tomorrow's pensions – important though that is. It is also whether big government itself will be able to survive as Europe's demographic window closes, whatever the outcome of today's financial crisis.

Second is the question of what Europe should do to maintain its workforce. Increasingly, we seem to be looking to migration to deal with shortages of labour or skills. But countries that depend on immigration can find themselves sucked into accepting ever greater numbers to sustain their economies, even if it is to the detriment of their own indigenous workforce. If European countries (including Britain) are to reduce their dependence on migrant labour they will have to reduce the demand for it, either by growing more slowly or by tackling the weaknesses and rigidities that bedevil their labour markets. Neither option will be easy, and a lot of what they entail will not be popular either.

Third, what can Europe do about its low fertility? For many women today, having fewer children than their mothers is one of feminism's achievements. They certainly do not want to be told to swap their briefcases for baking trays. Indeed, given what has happened to birth rates over the last 30 years, it is perhaps surprising that European women say they want to have children at all. Yet all the survey evidence on the subject shows not just that they do, but that in most countries they would like to have at least two children apiece. This is the paradox behind Europe's demographic dilemma. If the women of Europe, and especially those in the low fertility countries of Central, Southern and Eastern Europe, were to have the average of two children they say they would like, there would be no European population problem.

Fourth, European governments – and especially the larger ones – need to be realistic about the impact that their ageing and declining share of the global population will have on their place in the international pecking order. As others pull ahead, Europe's relative importance is bound to decline and the competitive pressures on us will inevitably increase, not just in economic terms but also diplomatically and militarily. Why should the world continue to accord the leading European powers (like Britain) the importance we have come to take for granted, when we will make up an ever smaller proportion of its population, economy and military muscle?

Fifth is the environmental impact of population change. In those parts of Europe where numbers are set to fall pressure on the environment should reduce, at any rate in theory. But even though Europe's population will be in decline that does not mean that, as far as climate change and pollution are concerned, we can expect to escape the problems caused by rapid population and economic growth elsewhere.

Looking at this list, one realises just how important the age and size of a country's population, and whether it is shrinking, stagnating or growing, is going to be over the next few decades. So how does Britain score? Our birth rate may be more buoyant than the European average, but the ability of our health and welfare systems to cope with an ageing society is dubious. Even before the credit crunch, the sustainability of our public finances was far more uncertain than any political leader or party was prepared to admit, particularly in view of Gordon Brown's huge spending spree when he was Chancellor. Our labour market could also be more efficient, and will have to be if we are to reduce immigration. As for our place in the world, that probably matters more to Britain – or at least to our ruling establishment – than it does to any other European country except France.

For almost 100 years from the middle of the 19th century Britain's demography was characterised by steadily falling fertility, and throughout the first half of the 20th century this was the cause of widespread concern. But for the last 50 years the course of the British population has been all over the place. First came the baby boom of the mid-'50s to early '70s, followed by an equally dramatic baby bust. Between 1965 and 1980 the TFR declined from over 2.8 children per woman in 1965 to just 1.7 by 1980. This was a huge and precipitate drop by any standards, from which the birth rate has only recently started to recover. To cap it all, we now also have an immigration boom. Perception, however, is taking a long time to catch up with reality. In the aftermath of the baby boom at home, and as numbers soared in the Third World, it was having too many children that people worried about. Today, the accepted view remains that having too large a population is the greater danger. Only in the last few years have people begun to think seriously again about the consequences of population decline.

If our demographic course over the last half century had been less bumpy, there is little doubt we would be facing fewer population-related problems today. Such an outcome, of course, cannot simply be dictated as a matter of policy. To that extent, those who argue that a detailed population policy could never work are right. But there is now a general acknowledgment that our demography is not going to be easy over the next few decades. There is also a growing realisation that allowing immigration to drive the British population to 70 million or more is likely to make matters worse rather than better. The Conservatives have spoken of having a population strategy. If by that they mean acknowledging more explicitly the role demography plays in many of the issues and problems we face, while at the same time trying to keep the balance of the population more stable, that should be an approach worth trying.

After a long period during which the power of numbers has been on Europe's side, we have to accept that it is beginning to work against us. This will be true even of those countries, like Britain, that are expected to escape an outright fall in their populations. The purpose of this book is to look at Britain's demographic prospects in the context of what is happening to population elsewhere in Europe and beyond, to set out the numbers and projections, examine the trends and issues behind them, and identify how we should try to deal with the opportunities and problems ahead.

1: Some History

I know no way of judging the future, except by the past.
Patrick Henry

Until 200 years ago, the population of the world grew remarkably slowly. Indeed for the first millennium AD it scarcely grew at all, increasing from around 230 million in Christ's day to 270 million a thousand years later.

But demography still made itself felt. The Roman Empire is often cited as the best known early example of population decline, helped on its way by a falling birth rate. The Emperor Augustus was so worried about the reluctance of his countrymen to breed that he instituted a series of what would now be called pro-natalist measures, including bachelor taxes on those who refused to wed.[10] But Augustus's laws did not work and nor did similar initiatives by his successors.

Hard data is understandably scarce, but historians reckon that Italy's population fell from a peak of seven million in AD1 to little more than half that in the 6th century.[11] In Rome itself the decline was even more marked. At the height of the empire, the city was reckoned to have a million inhabitants; by the 6th century it is thought to have been down to around 20,000 – a stark example of just how far a population can fall. We cannot be sure why the Romans stopped breeding, but loose morals, mass entertainment (those gladiator shows) and the pollution of the water supply have all been blamed at one time or another. All three have uncomfortable echoes for the Western world today. It was to take until the 12th century for the Italian population to recover to the level it had achieved at the height of the empire.

10 Parkin T, *Demography and Roman Society,* Johns Hopkins University Press, 1992
11 McEvedy C and Jones R, *Atlas of World Population History*, Facts on File, 1978

Across Europe generally the population is thought to have increased slowly until around 1,000AD when the expansion and improvement of agriculture inaugurated what might be termed the continent's first population explosion – albeit a modest one. Between 1000 and 1300 Europe's numbers are reckoned to have more than doubled to a record 80 million.[12]

In 1347 this benign era came to an abrupt end with the arrival of the Black Death. Over the next six years between a quarter and a third of the continent's population was wiped out by plague, and in Britain the figure was more like a half.[13] Plague and famine were to continue at a high level well into the 15th century. Even then numbers in many countries did little more than mark time right up to the beginning of the 18th century. England, which had seen its population fall from around four million before the Black Death to perhaps two million in 1400, did not regain its previous numbers until the mid-17th century.[14]

By 1800 Europe's population stood at 180 million. That was about the same as the Indian subcontinent but a lot less than China – which was then around 300 million. Overall, as the world entered the 19th century and embarked on the industrial era the global population stood at some 900 million, since when it has risen relentlessly to just under seven billion today.[15]

Across 19th century Europe, numbers really started to take off with industrialisation. Britain's population trebled between 1750 and 1850, and as other countries followed suit their populations, too, started to rise. Germany's numbers nearly trebled during the 19th century, while Italy's doubled over the same period.[16] The exception was France which, to the consternation of its leaders, grew much more slowly.

In 1800, France was Western Europe's most populous country by a considerable margin, outnumbering Britain by nearly 70%. Even the Germans, who were not to become a unified state until 70 years later, were fewer than the French. But by 1900, both the British and German populations had overtaken that of France.

12 McEvedy C and Jones R, *Atlas of World Population History*, Facts on File, 1978
13 ibid
14 ibid
15 ibid
16 ibid

France's decline from the superpower of Europe at the beginning of the 19th century to an also-ran a hundred years later was widely attributed to the slow growth of its population at a time when others were increasing exponentially. Indeed, well into the 20th century a growing population was held to be one of the crucial determinants of a country's economic and military power. Boosting one's numbers was considered an unequivocally good thing, while emigration supplied the raw material for Europe's expansion overseas.

When, towards the end of the century, European population growth slowed down it was the cause of widespread alarm, including in this country. In Britain the birth rate had been falling since the 1870s, even though the population continued to expand.[17] After the First World War, in which eight million European soldiers died, and the great flu pandemic of 1919, which claimed an even greater number of civilians, disquiet over population became even more pronounced.

Equally alarming to European politicians and pundits was that, just as the continent's population growth was slowing, in most of the rest of the world numbers were starting to accelerate – another echo of today. In 1800 Europe had accounted for roughly 20% of the world's population and during the 19th century its share increased. By 1900, out of a total world population of 1,650 million, one quarter was European.[18] Over the course of the 20th century this was to reduce dramatically, as other regions began to grow much faster. Between 1900-1950 Europe's population rose by what would now be considered a buoyant 35%. But over the same period numbers in every other region roughly doubled, except in Asia which grew by 50%.

However, the really big change in Europe's relative standing was to come in the second half of the century when, ironically, Europe's population was once again growing, thanks to the postwar baby boom. The 40% increase Europe managed between 1950 and 2000 had policymakers in some countries worrying about overcrowding, but it was dwarfed by what was happening elsewhere. As Asia, Africa and Latin America all

17 Mitchison R, *British Population Change Since 1860*, Macmillan 1977
18 McEvedy C and Jones R, op cit

grew by at least two-and-a-half times, and North America by 50%, Europe's share of world population at the start of the new millennium fell to just 12%, half of what it had been a hundred years earlier.

Emigration and Immigration

Ever since the tribes of Germany swept across the Roman Empire in the 5th century, Europe has been on the move. Between 800–1000 the Slavs moved into Russia and Eastern Europe, the Arabs seized chunks of the old Byzantine Empire, colonised Southern Spain and reached France, while the Vikings and other Nordic invaders made their presence felt in England and Holland.[19]

Next it was Western Europe's turn: the Normans invaded England, the Spanish drove out the Moors, the Venetians took much of the Western part of the Byzantine Empire, and the Germans and the Turks found themselves in competition for *Lebensraum* in Eastern Europe.

Up to then, religion had not generally been a factor in migration within Europe. This changed with the Reformation. At the end of the 16th century and during the first half of the 17th, 200,000 Huguenots left France, and 60,000 Protestants left the Netherlands.[20] Some of these religious refugees moved elsewhere in Europe, notably the Huguenots to England. Others went further afield, to the New World, which European explorers had already begun to open up.

In Latin America, the Spanish set a pattern that the English and French were to follow, not just in the Americas but also in Australasia. As the existing native populations were either wiped out or marginalised, they were replaced by waves of European settlers. By the 19th century, as its population soared, Europe began to export people on a scale that had never been seen before. In the 19th century, millions of Germans, Irish and Italians emigrated to the United States alone, as did many thousands of Russians, English, French, Swedes, Poles and others.

Millions also went to Latin America, especially Italians and Spanish, and in the 20th century millions more were to go to Australia, New

19 History of International Migration, University of Leiden, 2007; http://www.let.leidenuniv.nl/history/migration/chapter131.html

20 History of International Migration, University of Leiden, 2007; http://www.let.leidenuniv.nl/history/migration/chapter21.html

Zealand and Canada. Altogether, nearly 50 million people are reckoned to have left Europe between 1845 and 1914, ten times the total for the previous four centuries combined. Ten million of them came from the British Isles, although perhaps a third of these are thought to have later returned.

Emigration from Europe in the 19th and 20th centuries was primarily economic, but politics, war and disaster also featured. In the decade following the potato famine, two million Irish left for America, while 800,000 Germans went between 1866 and 1873, the years when Bismarck was unifying Germany.[21] Before the First World War two million Jews from Eastern Europe and Russia, also arrived in the US, driven out of their old countries by anti-Semitic pogroms.[22] In the 20th century at least another million Jews were to leave Europe for Israel after the horrors of the Second World War.

But emigration to the New World was not just a European affair; migration from Africa and Asia was also an important factor. Unlike its European counterpart, however, this was rarely voluntary. Between 1550, when the first slave ship sailed from Africa to the West Indies, and the gradual abolition of the trade in the 19th century, 15 million Africans are thought to have been taken to the New World.[23] By no means that many survived the journey, but today there are about 40 million African-Americans in the US and Caribbean, many descended from the 500,000 slaves forcibly removed there.[24]

Less well remembered is the system of indentured labour that superseded slavery, and which resulted in over two million Asians, largely from China and India, being shipped to work in European colonies around the world, mostly in the second half of the 19th century.[25] Supposedly these "coolies" were free men and women, although the conditions in which they travelled and worked were often little better than slavery. But at least

21 History of International Migration, University of Leiden, 2007; http://www.let.leidenuniv.nl/history/migration/chapter52.html#1

22 ibid

23 http://www.bbc.co.uk/worldservice/africa/features/storyofafrica/index_section9.shtml

24 http://www.slaveryinamerica.org/history/hs_es_overview.htm

25 Northrup D, *Indentured Labor in the Age of Imperialism, 1834-1922,* Cambridge University Press, 1995

those who survived usually had the option of returning home when their contracts expired. It is thought three quarters of the Indians who were transported in this way eventually went home. Perhaps this is why indentured labour is largely forgotten today.

Post 1945, Britain and France were broke and both also faced huge problems in their overseas empires, whose burgeoning populations were increasingly demanding independence. In countries as far flung as India and Algeria, European colonists found their privileged position under threat. When De Gaulle pulled out of Algeria in 1964, a million French *pieds noirs* fled back to the motherland in little more than a month.

Meanwhile across much of Europe, governments were wondering where the manpower would come from to rebuild their shattered economies. In Britain, fears of an inadequate workforce led to the establishment of both a National Advisory Committee on the Employment of the Elderly and a Royal Commission on Population.[26]

The Royal Commission sat for three years and produced a report which, with its various appendices and tables, ran to over 270 pages. No government since has attempted such a serious evaluation of the country's demography, and for that reason alone it makes fascinating reading. The commission was nothing if not comprehensive; among many other things, it considered the relationship between population and town planning, the impact of population growth on the balance of payments, what role the benefits system should play, the problems of an ageing society, and the impact of demography on Britain's military capability and role in the world.

Some of the things in the report would hardly cross our minds today. Britain's role as a source of immigrants for the Dominions was deemed sufficiently important to occupy several pages. But its main concerns still strike a chord, 60 years on. In particular, it warned that an ageing population would pose a growing problem for the welfare state, then in its infancy. Like everybody else, the commission failed to foresee the baby boom. But it was optimistic that if housing and welfare policies could be made more parent-friendly the birth rate could be encouraged modestly upwards. It certainly saw little, if any, need for immigration: "Continuous

26 Royal Commission on Population, Parliamentary Papers XIX, 1948-49

large scale immigration", it cautioned," would probably be impractical and would certainly be undesirable."

Little did the commission realise that, on this last point, it was already being overtaken by events. A year before its report came out in June 1949, the *SS Windrush* had docked at Tilbury and the first of what were to become many thousands of Caribbean immigrants had disembarked. Over the next decade, in a reversal of historic precedent, the colonies or ex-colonies of European powers began to send immigrants to their mother countries, even as whites continued to leave in search of a better life in North America, Australia and Southern Africa. For Britain this meant large influxes from the Caribbean and the Indian subcontinent. In France, it was Arabs from North Africa. In Germany, which had no colonial empire, migrants from Southern Europe and Turkey began to arrive in large numbers.

Boom and Gloom

Then in the mid-1950s, concern about the demographic outlook suddenly dissipated. Not only were immigrants available by the boat load to fill the jobs created by Europe's rapidly reviving economies, but the baby boom also took off. The baby boom is generally seen as flowing directly from the end of the Second World War. As peace was established, so the story goes, Europe's men returned home from the war and set about making up for six years' lost breeding. In fact, in Britain the birth rate had started rising in the late 1930s.[27] After an upward surge in 1946-47 it then dropped back again. It was not until the mid-'50s that birth rates took off in a sustained way, in Britain and elsewhere in the developed world. In many countries they actually peaked in the mid-'60s, a full 20 years after the war had ended.

What sparked off the baby boom was not so much the re-establishment of peace, as the return of prosperity and confidence of a sort that Europe had not known since before 1914. As rationing ended and full employment began to be taken for granted it really did seem, in Macmillan's famous observation of 1959, as if people had "never had it so good". Across the Western world, birth rates rose in response.

27 Mitchison R, op cit, p34

So sharp was the increase that, by the '60s, doomsayers were worrying that booming populations would lead to chronic overcrowding in the West and mass starvation in Asia and Africa. Robert MacNamara, then the US Defence Secretary, feared that population growth posed a bigger threat than nuclear war. Fortunately, it did not turn out that way. Thanks to the "green revolution", which dramatically boosted crop yields, the developing world learnt to feed itself. Famine, at least outside Africa, became largely a thing of the past. And while, in a high-tech age, demography no longer appeared to be of much military or strategic importance, in rapidly developing countries like India and China population growth came to be seen as one of the main drivers of economic development.

Then, as the pundits worried about over-population, demography took yet another sudden and unexpected turn. In both the West and the Soviet Union, fertility once again began to fall. At first, an easing of what was seen as population pressure was generally welcomed. Only when the fall in fertility turned into a protracted plunge did people wake up to the implications for economic growth and social security – particularly as life expectancy also began to increase dramatically.

Looking back across the demography of the last two millennia, several things stand out that are still relevant today:

- Despite two appalling wars, Europe's population rose by over a third in the first half of the 20th century.[28] Similarly, although famines in Russia, China, India and Africa killed tens of millions, they made little long term difference to the populations of any of these places.[29] In the modern world, the four horsemen of the apocalypse – war, famine, disease and death – no longer hold sway as they have done in earlier eras.

- The onset of industrialisation almost invariably results in both a drop in fertility and an increase in longevity. Once a country has been industrialised, mood and wellbeing seem to become important factors in

28 McEvedy C and Jones R, *Atlas of World Population History*, Facts on File, 1978
29 ibid

determining fertility. The return of prosperity was the main factor in the postwar baby boom. Conversely, when the collapse of communism led to a fall in living standards and job security across the old Eastern bloc, birth rates in most of those countries also collapsed.

- There is no law of man or nature that says that population should always go up. It has over the last 200 years. But over the longer term numbers have fallen as well as risen, and this has sometimes continued for quite long periods. Sometimes – and again for quite long periods – numbers have just stood still.

- Europe began the 20th century fretting over declining birth rates, spent the '60s and '70s worrying about the baby boom, and ended the century worrying again that fertility in many countries had fallen to levels that are unsustainably low. Not only can demographic trends change, they can also go full circle.

- Alarmed by global warming, environmentalists fear that the world is getting perilously close to its carrying capacity. But, although such fears certainly need to be taken seriously, it has not happened yet. Despite the huge increase in population since the industrial era began, and the huge rise in consumption that has accompanied it, the world has not yet run out of food or, indeed, any other raw material.

Sages Through the Ages

> No lesson seems to be so deeply inculcated by the experience of life as that you should never trust experts…They all require to have their strong wine diluted by a very large admixture of insipid common sense.
> Lord Salisbury

Comte's famous aphorism that demography is destiny has always struck a chord with the world's rulers and thinkers – even those who lived thousands of years ago. In classical times, the Greeks and the Romans both feared that they would die out unless they bred more. Contemporaries blamed the materialism of the day and the laziness of Greek and Roman men. Writing in 140BC, the historian Polybius complained that, "In our time all Greece was visited by a dearth of children and a general decay of population. This evil grew upon us rapidly, and without attracting attention, by our men becoming perverted to a passion for show and money and the pleasures of an idle life."[30]

Ironically, much the same complaint was being made at much the same time in Rome, even though the Roman Empire was still expanding, and was, in fact, just then absorbing the Greeks. In 131BC the censor Quintus Caecilius Metellus Macedonicus admonished his fellow citizens, "if we could survive without a wife, all of us would do without that nuisance. Since nature has so decreed that we cannot manage comfortably with them, nor live in any way without them, then we must plan for our lasting preservation rather than for our temporary pleasure."[31]

Quintus was a prescient man, but like many later demographic commentators he had a problem with timing. Rome did fall, and demography played a part in its demise, but the collapse was to take another 400 or 500 years. Today, being that far out would qualify as being wrong.

With the fall of Rome interest in the subject of population lapsed, as it did in most subjects, and only revived with the Enlightenment in the 18th century. The man generally credited with being the father of modern demography was the English clergyman, Thomas Malthus. By all accounts Malthus in person was kind, charming and mild mannered, but his name lives on as a byword for demographic pessimism. In 1798, as European populations were beginning to grow again after three centuries or more in the doldrums, Malthus published his *Essay on the Principle of Population,* in which he famously postulated that "population, when unchecked, increases in a geometrical ratio. Subsistence only increases in an arithmetical ratio." There would always, he went on, be "a strong and constantly operating check on population from the difficulty of subsistence".

30 Polybius, *The Histories,* Book XXXVI, Chapter 5

31 Quoted in Longman P, "The Return of Patriarchy", *Foreign Policy,* April 2006

Hunger, in Malthus view , was "a great restrictive law… and the race of man cannot, by any efforts of reason, escape from it." [32] Even at the time, it was a view that many found hard to accept. Inspired by the Enlightenment, a rival school of optimistic thinkers saw growing populations as a sign of wellbeing rather than a portent of famine. One of these so-called Utopians, whose work Malthus took special exception to, was William Godwin. Godwin declared that "myriads of centuries of still increasing population may pass away, and the earth be still found sufficient for the subsistence of his inhabitants."[33]

Today we still discuss Malthus, while Godwin is almost forgotten. Yet both have been proved right in their different ways. Famines and wars notwithstanding, Godwin's optimistic assessment of the earth's capacity to cope with larger populations has stood the test of time. But so, too, has Malthus's general view that large families are a major obstacle to removing poverty. Indeed, his call for "prudential restraint" – by which he meant later marriage – can be said to have opened the way for family planning.

By the end of the 19th century birth rates in most industrialised countries were falling, and the debate between Malthus and Godwin no longer seemed very relevant. Some 1500 years after the fall of Rome, worries about declining, rather than rising, populations were back on the agenda. Surprisingly, this happened first, not in Europe but in the United States. By 1900 the American birth rate was down 40% on a century earlier, while among the Wasps – the White Anglo-Saxon Protestants who ran the country – it had fallen even further.

That the US population was still growing rapidly thanks to massive immigration was small consolation to leading Wasps like the President, Theodore Roosevelt. In 1906 he used his State of the Union address to warn against "wilful sterility – the one sin for which the penalty is national death, race suicide". According to Roosevelt, part of the problem was due to what he carefully termed, in an interview with the *Ladies' Home Journal*, "the highly welcome emancipation of women". "This new freedom", he feared, "has been twisted into wrong where it has been taken to mean a

32 Malthus T, *An Essay on the Principle of Population*, Appleman P (ed), WW Norton, 1976
33 ibid

relief from all those duties and obligations which, though burdensome in the extreme, women cannot expect to escape."[34]

Much of what was written at the end of the 19th century and the beginning of the 20th century about the connection between growing wealth and falling birth rates would have been familiar to educated Greeks and Romans, nearly two millennia earlier. But there was one big difference: in the patriarchal societies of Greece and Rome, low fertility had been seen as an exclusively male problem. It was only in the early 20th century that the woman's attitude towards parenthood began to feature as a serious factor in demography.

In Europe, worries about low fertility peaked in the aftermath of the First World War and the great flu pandemic which followed. In *The Decline of the West*, published in 1918, Spengler predicted that Europe's population would decline for 200 years. Like Roosevelt, Spengler put much of the blame on the combination of growing wealth and female emancipation. Writing in *The Illustrated London News* in 1930, G K Chesterton was even gloomier: "If the recent decline in the birth rate were continued for a certain time," he warned, "it might end in there being no babies at all." The famous lament by the French demographer, Alfred Sauvy, that Europe's future would be one of "old people, in old houses, with old ideas" also dates from the 1930s.

Such thinking contributed to a raft of pro-natalist policies in France, as well as in fascist Germany and Italy, and communist Russia where Stalin banned abortion. It was at this time, too, that writers and policymakers first began to consider the implications of a falling population for a modern economy. In *Some Economic Consequences of a Declining Population*, written in 1935, John Maynard Keynes warned that "the first result to prosperity of a change over from an increasing to a declining population may be very disastrous." Interestingly, Keynes said nothing about the impact of population decline on pensions and social security, probably because both were so much less developed 70 years ago than they are now.

But after the Second World War, with the welfare state up and running and birth rates still subdued, the impact of an ageing population on social

34 "Mr Roosevelt's Views on Race Suicide", *Ladies' Home Journal,* February 1906

spending became a source of considerable official concern. In the late '40s, fears of an inadequate workforce in Britain led to the establishment of a National Advisory Committee on the Employment of the Elderly, as well as the Royal Commission on Population itself (see pp28). In 1954 the Phillips Committee warned, in terms that sound eerily familiar today, that by 1980 the dependency ratio of pensioners to workers would be unsustainable and that to deal with this the pension age should be raised by three years.[35]

Then, from the mid-50s the baby boom took off and the focus changed. Fascism had discredited pro-natalist policies in Europe (or at least the non-communist part of it) and there no longer seemed to be much connection between population and economic or even military power. In these buoyant circumstances, population was no longer a worry or a priority for the developed world.

In the developing world, it was a different matter. Alarmed by the gathering pace of population growth in the third world, a school of demographers dubbed the neo-Malthusians predicted in the late 60s that the rapid increase in the world's numbers would lead to mass starvation in developing countries and shortages of oil and other raw materials in the West.

Some of the claims made about population at the time were extraordinarily melodramatic. Paul Ehrlich, the most influential of the neo-Malthusians, famously warned in his 1968 book *The Population Bomb* that "in the 1970s and 1980s hundreds of millions of people will starve to death… At this late date nothing can be done to prevent a substantial increase in the world death rate…"[36] Among many other pronouncements, Ehrlich also declared that, if he were a betting man, he would not take odds on England surviving to the year 2000.

Fortunately, most of the neo-Malthusian's other alarmist predictions also failed to come to pass. Thanks to a combination of improved agricultural techniques and the extension of modern methods of birth control to even the poorest countries, hundreds of millions did not starve to death, although millions did go hungry. As the neo-Malthusians' star waned,

35 Report of the Phillips Committee on the Economic and Financial Problems of the Provision for Old Age, 1954

36 Ehrlich P, *The Population Bomb,* Pan Books, 1971

so another group of demographers came to prominence. The "cornucopian" school, as they were dubbed, believed strongly in the long-term
sustainability of humanity – much as Godwin had 200 years earlier.

The most prominent modern cornucopian was the American professor,
Julian Simon, whose books *The Ultimate Resource* (1981) and *The Resource-
ful Earth* (1984) argued that technological progress and human ingenuity
meant that there need be no level at which population would exceed the
world's carrying capacity. In the '80s and '90s, as the developed world
prospered on the back of the postwar baby boom and the developing
world learnt to feed itself, the cornucopians found themselves once again
in the ascendant.

But they, too, were not to have it all their own way for long. Mass
starvation might no longer be such a worry, but the same angst that had
driven the neo-Malthusians to prophesy global famine in the 1970s lies
behind many of the worries about global warming that preoccupy policymakers today. Meanwhile, as the new century dawned another old/new
trend was causing concern: fertility in most industrialised countries was
falling once again, and this time the process showed no sign of reversing
itself – if anything the opposite. Books like *The Empty Cradle* (2004) by
Phillip Longman warned that sub-replacement fertility would have a disastrous impact on advanced societies. With populations ageing, stagnating and even shrinking across the developed world, the outlook suddenly
seemed much less benign than the cornucopians had thought.

So who are we to believe? All three schools of thought have their insights, but none can claim complete vindication. For declinists like Longman, the trends certainly seem to be going their way. But half a century
ago their predecessors were badly caught out by the baby boom. At the
other end of the scale, the cornucopian view, that somehow or other we
will all muddle through, turns out to be pretty much what we have done.
But while this may be what Lord Salisbury meant by "a large admixture of
common sense", it hardly counts as forecasting. And, just at the moment,
with pressure mounting on supplies of energy and most raw materials
around the world, it is not quite as reassuring as it was either.

As for the Malthusians, it is easy to mock them for getting their dire
prophesies so wrong (and, touch wood, so far they always have been

wrong). But we should not forget that it was Malthus who first advocated the "prudent restraint" of population, which is now taken for granted nearly everywhere. What is new, and makes a commentator's work harder, is that with some countries and continents still growing extraordinarily rapidly and others already starting to decline, today all three schools of thought can point to some current trends or factors to back up their position.

2: The Intricacies of Demography

The art of prophecy is very difficult, especially with respect to the future.
Mark Twain

A huge amount of effort goes into compiling the demographic figures and forecasts on which policymakers and more general commentators (like this one) rely as they seek to divine what is going to happen next, and what they should be trying to do or say about it. Most countries produce demographic statistics and projections, as do various international bodies, academic institutions and think tanks. But by far the most widely used forecast is the medium fertility variant world population projection produced by the UN population bureau.

Every two years this group re-examines the demographic prospects up to 2050 for every country, using a range of fertility assumptions from high to low, as well as data on current birth and immigration rates. Its central projection is then embodied in the medium fertility variant projection. It is important to stress that the medium fertility variant is neither flawless nor infallible. Some of the assumptions it makes about Europe are certainly optimistic, and that may well be true of other continents as well. But the UN is the only body whose demographers cover all countries, comprehensively and using the same methodology. For these reasons, the medium fertility variant is the figure most often used by policymakers and commentators around the world. Unless otherwise stated the revised 2008 series, released in March 2009, will be the one used in this book.

The skill in making demographic projections lies in getting the right combination of past experience, current trends and recent data; used in combination, they are a powerful set of tools. Keeping the data up to date is also important because demographic trends can change, as we have seen, and indeed do so the whole time. But demographers also now go one step further and try to anticipate changes in trends, even before they occur. For this they rely heavily on a model of demographic transition which first emerged in Europe in the 19th century, and has held good – more or less – for all countries that have industrialised since.

Demographic Transition

> *Consistency is contrary to nature, contrary to life.*
> Aldous Huxley

The first big demographic transition is thought to have taken place 8,000 years ago when man ceased to be a hunter-gatherer, settled down to primitive farming, and his numbers rose.[37] A modern demographic transition is more complex, not least because greater numbers are involved, but essentially it follows the same pattern. As a country develops, its death rate drops due to better nutrition. Then, as mortality stabilises, birth rates begin to fall, thanks usually to the introduction of birth control and increasing female participation in the labour force. The result of these shifts is a period of rapid population growth, lasting perhaps two generations, during which birth rates decline more slowly than death rates, as people live longer. Then, as birth rates fall, equilibrium is re-established and population growth slows.

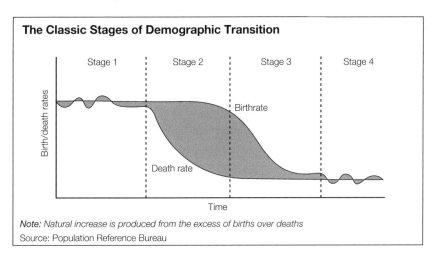

The Classic Stages of Demographic Transition

Note: Natural increase is produced from the excess of births over deaths
Source: Population Reference Bureau

37 Livi-Bacci M, *A Concise History of World Population,* 3rd edition, Blackwell, 2001

It was not until the 1930s and '40s that demographers realised that a modern demographic transition had got underway with the onset of the Industrial Revolution, 200 years before. From the mid-18th to the late 19th centuries, huge improvements, first in food supply and then in health and hygiene, led to dramatic increases in population across most of Western Europe, and later North America and Russia as well.[38] Today, very much the same thing is happening across Latin America, Asia and the Middle East, although the pace of change varies significantly between regions, and even from country to country within the same region.

It happened first, though, in Britain, and it is on our experience that the classic model of demographic transition is based. Here the death rate began to fall at the end of the 18th century, as the benefits of the agricultural revolution and then better sanitation and other public health measures, fed through. Birth rates, however, remained at their old, high level until contraception began to be available from the 1870s onwards. Only then, a hundred years after the death rate had begun to decline, did the birth rate also fall.[39]

It is this model that underlies most attempts at population forecasting today. But demographers disagree about how closely today's developing countries will follow the classical Western model as they make their own transitions. And in the West, itself, stability remains worryingly elusive as birth rates stick at levels that would have seemed inconceivable just a few decades ago, and longevity increases apace.

Living for Ever?

> *The days of our age are three score years and ten: and though men be so strong that they come to four score years: yet is their strength then but labour and sorrow.*
> Psalm 90

Even today most of humanity fails to make the psalmist's three score years and ten. According to the UN, life expectancy across the globe

38 Rostow WW, *The Great Population Spike and After,* Oxford University Press, 1998
39 Crouzet, *The Victorian Economy,* Routledge, 2005

will not reach 70 until the end of the next decade. But in the developed world it is already far higher and still increasing rapidly – so rapidly, in fact, that pensions and health systems in all advanced countries are finding it hard to cope.

The irony is that living longer should be a cause for celebration not consternation, especially since we are managing to stay healthy and active for longer as well. In Shakespeare's time, average life expectancy was about 25-30.[40] By 1798, when Malthus was alerting the world to the danger (as he saw it) of exponential population growth, it had risen to around 35. Over the last 30 years the increase in longevity has been almost as startling as the decrease in fertility – especially for men.

In 1976, life expectancy for a British woman was 76 and 70 for a man. Today the figures are 82 and 77 respectively. For a British man life expectancy has increased by an extraordinary 2.5 years over the last decade alone, which equates to an extra 15 minutes for every hour survived. How long this longevity spurt can go on, no one knows. The current demographic consensus is that life expectancy will continue to increase, but at a slower pace. In developed countries life expectancy by 2030 is projected to be three or four years more than it is today, which in Britain's case would mean 84 for a woman and nearly 80 for a man.

But the notion that society is suddenly ageing so fast because longevity has increased is half the story at most. Living longer only pushes the average age up to a significant (and problematic) extent if, at the same time, there are fewer young people to reduce the average. Ageing is just as much about this, as it is about life expectancy. The main reason European countries today are ageing so rapidly is low fertility, not increased longevity.

Compare the prospects of the US and China, 25 years down the road. Mainly because the US fertility rate is significantly higher than China's and expected to remain so, China will age much more rapidly than America. At the moment just 8% of the Chinese population is aged over 65, compared with 13% in the US. But by 2035 this gap will have virtually disappeared, with the figure for China projected to be 19.2% compared to 20.6% for the US. At the moment, too, the Chinese have a lower median age at 34, than the Americans at 36. But by 2035 that is expected to reverse, with the median age in the US projected to be 40 compared with 43 in China.

Yet despite China having aged so much faster than the US as a society, Americans will still be more long-lived; in 2035 life expectancy in the US is projected to be 81, compared with 78 by then in China. For any society or country fertility is the key to ageing. Across Europe the average fertility rate is lower even than China's. That is why we are ageing faster than both, why our dependency ratios are collapsing, and why our pensions system is in trouble.

Fertility and Population Momentum

> *Jeannie, Jeannie, full of hopes, /Read a book by Marie Stopes, /But to judge from her condition, /She must have read the wrong edition*
> Children's doggerel from the 1920s

Traditionally, demographers measured fertility in terms of a country's annual birth rate, expressed as the number of live births per thousand of population. Nowadays they normally use the total fertility rate (TFR). This is not a measurement as such, but a calculation of the total number of children an average woman is likely to have in her lifetime based on current birth rates. For a population to replace itself, it needs a TFR of at least 2.1 children per woman.

On either basis, fertility has been falling in nearly all countries, not just the industrialised West, since at least the 1970s. Even in Africa the total fertility rate has declined from 6.6 children 30 years ago, to 4.6 today. In Latin America the figure has dropped from 4.5 in the mid-70s to 2.25 today, and in Asia from just over 4.0 to slightly below 2.5.

Experience suggests that, all other things being equal, as a country develops its fertility usually falls. If children do not have to be sent to school, they are a source of cheap labour. Once they have to be educated, they become a cost rather than an asset, and both fertility rates and the number of children per family soon fall. The next stage comes when women start using birth control to plan the size of their families and free them to find employment outside the home, at which point fertility can be expected to take another downward turn.

In many developing countries, fertility overall has already fallen to replacement level or below. This is true not just of China, with its one
child policy, but also, of Brazil, Thailand and Iran, to name but a few.
Economic development has played a large part in this, just as the classical
model of demographic transition suggested it would, and so has the spread
of educational opportunities for women.

In Brazil, for instance, total fertility fell from 6 in 1966 to 2.5 children
per woman in 1996. But while the figure for women with no education
was 5, for those with primary schooling it was 3.3, and for those with
secondary schooling it was 2.1, or replacement level. For the elite, with
tertiary education, it was a sub-replacement 1.5.[41]

All of this is well documented. But the theory of demographic transition also predicted that, at some point, fertility would stop declining.
Until recently, the assumption was that this would happen at or around
the replacement rate of 2.1 children per woman. What demographers did
not foresee, even 20 years ago, was that in many countries fertility would
not just undershoot the replacement rate, but remain at stubbornly low
levels thereafter.

About 40% of the world's population now live in countries in which
women have so few children that the population is set to decline over the
long term. In some countries fertility has now fallen to a level that would
have been inconceivable 50 years ago, and shows little, if any, sign of recovering. In others, as has already been noted, it has crept up over recent
years. Even so the only country in Europe that still has a TFR of 2.1 is
Iceland. In places as diverse as Italy, Poland, Bulgaria, Germany and Japan
the current TFR is at or below 1.4 children per woman. Such low fertility has led to speculation that the developed world has now embarked on
another demographic transition, in which the pressures and pleasures of
contemporary life have finally overcome the natural urge to reproduce.

In countries afflicted by very low fertility three factors currently mask
what is happening. First, the baby boom generation is still in charge, and
– more importantly – still working. Second, increasing longevity means
that despite low fertility the population has not yet started to fall. Third,

41 Lutz W, Sanderson W and Scherbov S (eds), *The End of World Population Growth in the 21st Century*, Earthscan, 2004

many countries are sucking in large numbers of immigrants to counterbalance the deficiency in their own numbers.

In the developing world, meanwhile, falling fertility is masked by overall population growth. Women in these countries are having fewer children than was the case even 15 years ago, but the built-in momentum of their young populations means that numbers are still rising. This is known as population momentum, and in many developing countries it is the most important influence on future population.

In Iran, for instance, overall numbers are projected to grow from 70 million today to over 95 million by mid-century, even though the latest figure for the country's TFR is now below replacement level. But until a few years ago it was much higher: in just 20 years it has fallen from over six children per woman in the mid-'80s to below two today. Because the proportion of young people in the Iranian population is still disproportionately high, as they have children (albeit at a far lower rate than their parents) the population will continue to grow for decades to come, but at a slowing pace.

Further down the line, if fertility plunges substantially below replacement rate and stays there, then eventually population momentum will go into reverse. This has not happened yet, but in Europe it could soon be a real threat to those countries that are now entering their second generation of very low fertility.

The Tempo Adjusted TFR

Some demographers have sought to refine the TFR by making an allowance in its calculation for the postponement of childbearing that has taken place in most developed countries over recent decades, and especially in Europe. The theory is that postponement can result in a decline in the number of births in a given year, which depresses the conventional TFR. But if women are merely postponing having children rather than foregoing them, then the total number they have during the course of their lifetime should not change. The proponents of the so-called "tempo adjusted TFR" point out that on this basis, the fertility of many of the very low-fertility countries in Europe is higher than the standard TFR suggests, while for France and Ireland it would be at or even above replacement rate.

Do such arguments add up? Postponement clearly has been an important factor in the dramatic drop in the TFRs of the very low fertility countries over the last quarter of a century. The impact it has had is examined in Chapter 5. However postponement is only one part of the story, and eventually it should either slow or stop altogether. Because of this not all demographers accept that the tempo adjusted TFR is a more reliable guide than the conventional measure.

In this book the figure given for any particular TFR will be those produced by the UN, on the conventional basis.

Can We Trust the Projections?

> *The future ain't what it used to be.*
> Yogi Berra

For a book based on projections, in many ways this is the biggest question of all. Demographers may rely on statistics rather than crystal balls, but as Ehrlich and his followers demonstrated in such spectacular fashion in the 1970s, this does not mean that they will be proved right.

A more eminent sage, J M Keynes, was also caught out by demography (albeit he was an economist not a demographer). Speaking about population decline in 1937, he opined that "perhaps the most outstanding example of a case where we have a considerable power of seeing into the future is the prospective trend of population."[42] The Government of the day thought so, too. So worried were ministers by the apparently inexorable decline of the birth rate that they introduced a Population (Statistics) Bill to help them find out what was going on. Here is the Minister of Health, Sir Kingsley Wood, proposing its second reading in November 1937; much of what he said then sounds eerily familiar today:

---

42 Keynes JM, *The General Theory and After*, Moggridge D (ed), The Royal Economics Society, Macmillan, 1973, p125

Anxiety as to the future trend of population is growing in many nations in Europe today. So far as our own country is concerned, until recently the trend has been unmistakable, and if we accepted certain assumptions our population would fall in 30 years to 35,000,000 and in 100 years to 5,000,000. From 1871-1933 the birth rate has steadily declined. In 1871 it was 35 per thousand of the population; in 1901 it had dropped to 28; by 1921 it had further declined to 22; and in 1933 it had reached the low figure of 14. Thus since 1871 the birth rate in this country has more than halved itself.

Another factor of importance that I desire to bring before the House is that it is probable that our population in the immediate future will contain a much larger proportion of older people. On the other hand it is true that since the birth rate reached its lowest level in 1933, it has... remained without further decline and with a slight upward tendency. Too much must certainly not be built upon this....

Like everyone else, both Keynes and Sir Kingsley completely failed to foresee the great post-war baby boom which started 15 years later. By 1967 the birth rate was back up to 18 per thousand and, far from falling to 35 million as Sir Kingsley feared, the population of the UK had just topped 55 million.

To a greater or lesser extent most population projections turn out to be wrong in the event, for the simple reason that their components change. But that does not mean we should disregard them. By showing us the likely outcome if present trends continue unchanged, they help us both to prepare for the future and to decide what we should try to do to influence it. As to their accuracy, what matters is what components change and by how much. The huge increase in migration has recently complicated matters in this country, because migration, as has already been noted, is the most changeable factor of all. It can be turned on and off in a matter of a year or two, and often is. But migrants apart, the number of pensioners over the next 60 years can be projected with reasonable confidence because they have already been born, likewise, with the number of indigenous workers over the next 20 years.

The UN demographers whose figures this book uses accept that they are projecting a moving picture, which is why they revise their figures every two years. In the 1990s they predicted that the world's population this century would top 11 billion; now they are projecting just over 9 billion. Most significant of all, in this respect, is the UN's projection that, by mid-century the majority of countries will have converged on an average fertility rate of around 2.00 children per woman – marginally below replacement level.

For most developed countries, the UN assumption is that the current sharp decline in fertility will slow from now on and then reverse, so that by 2050 the average TFR across the developed world will be 1.8 children per woman. For less developed countries, the UN projection is that their TFR will continue to decline from an average 2.75 today to just over 2.00 by mid-century. From this stems its central conclusion that, by the end of the century, the world's population will have stabilised and may even have started to fall.

These long-term projections about global fertility need to be taken with a large pinch of salt. There is, for instance, no strong reason for thinking fertility in developing countries will stop at 2.00 rather than continue on down as it has in most Western counties. Meanwhile, in the developed world virtually no one expects fertility to return to the replacement rate in the very low fertility countries of Southern, Eastern and Central Europe.

However, if birth rates remain at the sort of levels seen in Japan and some parts of Europe during the last decade, the fall in the population of some of the very low fertility countries could be catastrophic. In a set of long-term predictions for the world population up to 2300, published in 2003, the UN made this point to justify its belief that European fertility levels must eventually recover later this century. If they stayed at current levels, the report pointed out:

> *By 2300, Western, Southern and Northern Europe would each have only 28-30 million people, and Eastern Europe would have only 5 million. The European Union...would fall by 2300 to only 59 million. About half the countries of Europe would lose 95 per cent or more*

*of their population, and such countries as the Russian Federation and
Italy would have only 1 per cent of their population left. Although one
might entertain the possibility that fertility will never rise above current
levels, the consequences appear sufficiently grotesque as to make this
seem improbable.*

This is obviously a reduction to absurdity, but it is true that things that
can't go on forever usually don't. In Europe generally fertility rates have
started to edge up again from their recent record lows. In Britain, the
Government Actuary's Department assumes that the fertility rate will
stabilise at around 1.8, a figure that it surpassed in 2007 for the first time in
over 30 years.[43] Much the same has happened in France and the US, the
Western world's two big demographic success stories where fertility has
recovered from 1.7 in the '70s to near replacement now. So perhaps fertility will recover significantly in other parts of Europe as well. But there
is little, if any, sign of it at the moment and many authorities, including
the European Commission, doubt that it will (see Chapter 4).

All in all, the UN's projection that, across most of the world, fertility will stabilise at just below replacement level by mid-century should
be taken for what it is, a best-guess – a well informed one, certainly,
but nonetheless a guess. Events, natural and manmade, can also upset
the demographers' projections. The First World War and the Great
Depression lowered birth rates across the Western world. The return
to stability and prosperity after the horrors of the 1930s and '40s led
on to the post-war baby boom. The current decline in European birth
rates, although it started in the late '60s, really took off after the oil
shock of 1973.

More recently, the collapse of communism has had a devastating effect
on the demography of the former Soviet Union. In Southern Africa, Aids
has brought previously rapid population growth to a halt. On the whole
though, it is not so much famine and disease that affect birth and death
rates today, but the psychological factors which shape people's confidence
in the future.

43 http://www.gad.gov.uk/Demography_Data/Population/index.asp?v=Table&pic=2006|uk|tfrcfs

With so many trends and events to contend with, demography can never be a precise science. Inevitably, the further forward it attempts to peer the less sure it becomes. And, as with economic forecasting, overall demographic trends are easier to divine than the particular. But while it is rare for a population projection to prove spot on over a very long period the trends, at least for the next quarter of a century, are already pretty clear – if only because most of the people who will be alive during the period have already been born.

Until 2035, and probably for another 20 years beyond, the pattern of ageing and then falling populations in advanced, mainly developed countries, and sharply rising, youthful populations across the developing world will continue. Looking still further into the future it seems likely that after 2050 populations will age and then begin to decline right across the globe, with the exception of the least developed countries in Africa and the Middle East – although even there demographic growth will eventually slow down. As a result, in the last quarter of this century the overall global population could well begin to decline for the first time since the Middle Ages.

3: What is going to happen?

Counting Heads

Every moment dies a man, / Every moment one is born.
Tennyson

Every moment dies a man, / Every moment 1 $^{1}/_{16^{th}}$ is born.
Charles Babbage, parodying Tennyson

A much fuller explanation of the projections for Europe and the world can be found in the Appendix. It lays out not just the numbers, but also the factors behind them and looks at what their consequences might be. Below is a briefer summary of the main trends in the key countries and regions, as identified by the UN.

Globally, population growth over the next 25 years is projected to be slightly slower than over the last 25 in terms of overall numbers, and significantly lower in percentage terms. Between 1980 and 2005, mankind increased by just over two billion or roughly 45%. Between 2005 and 2030, the UN is projecting a further rise of 1.8 billion, or 27.5%.

Across the Americas, Africa and Australasia populations are expected to continue growing strongly up to mid-century and probably beyond. In Asia the picture is mixed; most countries will keep growing and, taking the continent as a whole, numbers will keep increasing. However, in China the population should stop rising in around 25 years time, and in Japan it is already declining. And in Europe, even allowing for immigration, numbers are expected to peak within the next decade.

But it will not just be raw numbers that determine a nation's place in the new demographic hierarchy. Even more important will be how sustainable a country's population turns out to be. Here, the UN projections are doubly useful. Not only do they show where the most significant population gains and losses are expected, they also provide an early indicator of whether these are likely to prove a boon or a burden for any particular country.

Asia

As the West wanes so the nations of the East will wax, or so popular wisdom has it and looking at the likes of China and India one can see why. For years, China's growth has overshadowed all of its competitors', and it is still comfortably the world's most populous nation. Between 1950 and today, its population more than doubled, from 550 million in 1950 to over 1.3 billion in 2005. Mao saw population as a source of strength, but subsequently the dangers of such exponential growth led the authorities to introduce the famous one-child policy (OCP). Births fell from 21 million a year in the 1970s, when the population was some 500 million less, to around 18 million today. Largely as a result of the OCP China's population is now expected to peak at a bit under 1.5 billion in 2035, a relatively modest increase of some 10% on its current level.

The OCP, however, is not as all-encompassing as it sounds. China's TFR is, in fact, around 1.8 children per woman, mainly because the policy only really applies to urban families. The OCP also has its pitfalls, not least that the ubiquitous desire to bear a male heir has resulted in a heavily skewed gender ratio. A problem the world over, the usual ratio is 107 boys for every 100 girls; in China, according to the UN, it has reached 120 boys for every 100 girls. As its population growth slows right down, China will also inevitably age very rapidly, as has already been discussed. For a country with little conception of state welfare, the prospect of 280 million people of pensionable age in 2035, and rising fast, must be cause for serious concern. Demographers joke that China will grow old before it grows rich, and a quick look at its population projections shows why.

Meanwhile India, Asia's other giant, continues to grow apace, so much so that the Tiger is on course to overhaul the Dragon as the world's most populous nation as early as 2025. By 2035 India's population is projected to reach 1,525 million, and over 1,600 million by 2050. But the main difference between the two is not that India will soon have even more people than China, but that its population growth has been smoother.

When Indira Gandhi tried to introduce compulsory birth control in the 1970s she soon lost office and ever since, although Indian fertility has slowed, it has done so at a far more moderate rate than in China. As a result, India will remain a very young country for decades to come. Provided it can keep up its recent rate of economic growth this should be an enormous advantage, but if the pace slackens it could all too easily turn into a threat. By 2035 just 10% of its population will be over 65, and for the foreseeable future it will have an army of workers waiting in the wings.

As India and China duel for population supremacy, Japan increasingly finds itself cast as the bogeyman of Asian demographics. After decades of very low fertility, the land of the rising sun has more in common with the potential population basket cases of Southern and Eastern Europe, than its main Asian competitors. Japan's population has just begun to fall, and by 2035 it is expected that it will have declined to less than 114 million compared with 127 million in 2005. Japan already has the oldest population in the world; by 2035 32% of Japanese will be over 65, with just two workers to support each pensioner.

Even immigration seems unlikely to be able to plug the looming demographic deficit: Japan is almost entirely ethnically homogenous; of a population of 128 million, just 1.5 million are foreign born.[44] Japanese immigration has risen recently, but even so it currently averages just 30,000 a year. That compares with 330,000 a year in Italy, which has a similar demographic profile. But an influx of migrants to prop up Japan would, it is generally accepted, cause too much uproar to be politically acceptable.

The Americas
Across the Pacific, the demographic prospects of the United States could hardly be more different from Japan's. For a developed country, it is remarkable how the US has avoided the population quicksand that is fast engulfing much of the rest of the industrialised world. Life expectancy is much the same as in other developed nations, but the key to America's

---

44 Statistics Japan, 2005 Census; http://www.stat.go.jp/english/data/kokusei/2005/kihon1/00/hyodai.htm

demographic buoyancy is its consistently high fertility rate. After bottoming out at 1.8 in the early 1980s, the TFR has since recovered to 2.1 – bang on the theoretical replacement rate.

In large part this demographic buoyancy can be attributed to the growing Hispanic community, the fertility of which far outpaces that of any other group. Together with high and consistent immigration (also mostly Hispanic), this has helped put the US population on course to hit 380 million by 2035, some 25% above today's level. And with just 20% of the population expected to be over 65 by then, America's dependency ratio will be far better than any of its competitors in Europe. While Europe will be losing people of working age (defined as 15-64) over the next 25 years America will add 35 million, bringing the total to over 235 million and a robust 62% of the population.

South of the Rio Grande, the story is much the same as in the US. Populations continue to grow rapidly, although the pace is slowing. Latin America's fertility has now fallen to around replacement level and the median age is 27. By 2035 it is projected to be 36, which, while a sharper increase, will still be youthful by the standards of North America or Europe. By then, the regional giant Brazil expects to see its numbers rise from 186 million in 2005 to over 220 million people, while Mexico is projected to climb from 105 to 129 million.

Africa and the Middle East

In North Africa and the Middle East fertility has fallen by some 40% over the last 25 years. But it remains well above replacement level and this, combined with increasing longevity and strong population momentum, means that numbers in both regions will continue to grow rapidly for decades to come. It is thanks to its impressive TFR of 2.9 that Egypt is projected to reach 116 million by 2035 from 77 million in 2005. Also by 2035 the Palestinian Territories and Yemen should see their numbers double from their 2005 level.

In sub-Saharan Africa the population more than doubled to over 750 million between 1975 and 2005 and this pace looks set to continue, putting a huge strain on economies and resources across the continent. The scale of the growth expected in these countries over the next decade alone was given in the introduction. Taking a longer view, between 2005 and 2035 the region's population is projected to rise from 765 million to 1,422 million. Nigeria, Africa's most populous nation is projected to add 100 million people over this period, bringing it to 243 million. By 2035 there also expected to be 140 million Ethiopians and 120 million Congolese, which will be an increase of 70 million and 60 million respectively.

The biggest threat to the continued exponential growth of African populations is Aids. In South Africa, the disease has led to a horrifying collapse in life expectancy, down from 61 in 1990 to 51 today. Because of Aids, South Africa's population is expected to increase by just seven million between 2005 and 2035, to 55 million, despite its high birth rate.

With a median age in the early twenties, most countries in Africa and the Middle East are also very young, and set to stay that way for decades to come. This could be their greatest asset, but without jobs for the burgeoning number of unemployed it could instead turn into a huge liability.

Europe

One hundred years ago, a quarter of the world's population was European, but by 2000 it was down to 12% and this relative decline is set to continue. It is not so much that Europe has been shrinking – at least not yet – but that others have been growing faster. Since 1950 Europe's population (the whole continent, not just the EU) has risen steadily from 550 million to approximately 730 million today.

But in the next few years Europe's numbers are expected to peak, with the UN projecting a steady decline from 2015 even allowing for immigration. By 2035 the continent's overall population is expected to be back down to around 715 million, or 8% of the global total. Considering that European fertility has been below replacement level for over 30 years, and now hovers around 1.5 children per woman, it is perhaps surprising that its population is not shrinking even faster. One factor sustaining it, at least for a few decades, is longevity. Across Europe, life expectancy has risen from 66 in 1950 to 76 today. By 2035 it is projected to reach an impressive 80 years. The natural consequence of increasing longevity should be a rise in the overall population, as indeed it was during the latter part of the 20th century.

In Europe today, however, because fewer deaths are being accompanied by fewer births, it is more likely to lead to ageing stagnation. By 2035 Europe's population is projected to drop by just 2%, but over the same period the average age will rise from an already high 39 to 46 – an increase of nearly 20%. The impact this will have on welfare and pension systems is already the cause of huge concern. In 1950 just 8% of Europeans were pensioners; this has now doubled to 16%, and is set to reach 25% by 2035. By then there are projected to be 173 million Europeans aged 65 or more and 440 million aged 15-64 to support them, 60 million fewer than today.

Before we all get too alarmed, however, two important caveats should be entered. The first is that, while the projections for Europe overall are undeniably scary, we are not all in the same boat. The figures given above are for the whole continent, which means they include the European components of the former Soviet Union, including Russia, Ukraine and Belarus. As has already been mentioned, for all three of these countries,the demographic prognosis is especially alarming. Russia's population is already declining at the rate of 10,000 a week. Having fallen from 148 million at its peak in 1990 to around 143 million in 2005, it is on course to fall to 125 million by 2035. The outlook for Ukraine and Belarus is even starker, with both projected to lose about 20% of their population over the same period.

All three have extremely low TFR's, but what differentiates them from the other very low fertility countries is their high mortality rates. Astonishingly life expectancy in these countries has not only failed to rise over the last few decades, as it has virtually everywhere else in the world, but actually fallen. In 1960 male life expectancy in Russia was 64, which was meagre enough. Now that has fallen to under 59, as alcohol, poverty, collapsing health care and Aids all take their toll.

Strip out Europe-wide figures like these, and the outlook for the 27 countries that make up the EU looks if not exactly comfortable, at least better. Thanks entirely to rising longevity and immigration (and mainly the latter), the European Commission predicts that population of the EU27 will rise from 499 million today, to a peak of 521 million in 2035 before falling back to 515 million in 2050.[45] The 2008 UN figures have it rising from 490 million in 2005 to 504 million in 2035 and then sliding to around 490 million in 2050. But on either set of projections the EU will soon start to age rapidly, whatever the pace of immigration. By 2035 a quarter of its population is projected to be over-65 and the ratio of pensioners to children will be two to one.

The second caveat is that within the EU there are marked differences, first between the former communist states that joined in 2004 and the rest, and second between the very low fertility countries of Central, Southern and Eastern Europe and those in the North and West (including Britain) whose prospects look more sustainable. While every EU country will age, not all of them will shrink. In the North-West corner of the continent, France, Britain, Ireland, the Netherlands, Sweden and Luxembourg all look set to buck the trend of falling numbers. France recently announced with great fanfare that its fertility rate had again reached two children per woman, putting it on a par with Ireland in the EU. The British TFR has also risen steadily over the last five years, with the latest (2007) figure showing it at 1.9 and the UN putting it at 1.85.[46]

At the other end of the scale, the situation in Eastern Europe looks dire, with the population of many countries in the region already in decline. Here, the fall of the Berlin Wall in 1989 marked a demographic turning point as fertility plunged from around replacement level during the communist era to 1.3 or even less in the 1990s. In addition life expectancy, at just 69 today, remains six years below the European average. This combination of low life expectancy and low fertility (plus high emigration, at least recently) means that the population of the ten former communist EU members is projected to fall by over eight million in total, between now and 2035, and by 16 million by 2050.

45 Population Projection, Eurostat; http://epp.eurostat.ec.europa.eu/portal/page?_page-id=1996,39140985&_dad=portal&_schema=PORTAL&screen=detailref&language=en&product=REF_TB_population&root=REF_TB_population/t_popula/t_proj/tps00002

46 http://www.statistics.gov.uk/cci/nugget.asp?ID=951

More details for individual countries are given in the Appendix. In virtually all cases, however, the crucial determinant of any European country's demographic prospects between now and mid-century will be the interaction between fertility and immigration. This can be clearly seen in the projections for the largest European states, but it applies equally to the middle-sized and small ones as well.

Thus Germany, Europe's largest country, not only has very low fertility at less than 1.4 children per woman, but is also projected to receive only a little over 100,000 immigrants a year. In terms of the size of its population this is low by European standards and, together with its low birth rate, is the reason that its population is projected to start falling both soon and rapidly.

Italy, on the other hand, has three-quarters of the population of Germany, equally low fertility but over three times as many immigrants. After 30 years of very low birth rates Italy is often cited as the continent's demographic basket case. But, as far as overall numbers are concerned, its poor fertility is now being more than offset by immigration running at over 300,000 a year for the past decade. So while it had been thought that the Italian population would shrink between now and mid-century, in the latest projections it is set to level peg – entirely due to immigration.

Spain is another example of a country using immigration to offset a low birth rate, but in its case the numbers involved are even larger. Between 2000-2005 immigration into the country topped more than 500,000 a year. This has now dropped to 350,000 a year, and is projected to fall further to under 200,000 by the 2020s. Even so, the overall result is that Spain's population, which like Italy's had been expected to fall, is now projected not just to hold its own but to rise quite rapidly from 43 million in 2005 to over 50 million by mid-century.

By contrast, France has comparatively low immigration, at around 100,000 a year, but its fertility at nearly two children per woman is far higher than the European average. As a result, between 2005 and 2035 the French population is expected to rise by 10% from 61 to 67 million.

Britain

Britain and France have almost identically sized populations, and in the last few years our TFR has been almost as high. But our level of immigration is almost double theirs, and because of this our population is now projected to grow substantially faster.

The latest figures from the Government Actuary's Department (GAD), the body responsible for Britain's population projections, show the UK population rising rapidly from 61 million today to 71 million by 2031, and then continuing more slowly to 75 million by 2050.[47] This would make us one of the fastest growing countries in the EU, outpaced only by Ireland, Luxembourg and (ironically) Spain. The UN uses a slightly lower assumption for immigration than the GAD. Its projection is a UK population of just over 69 million by 2035 and 72.4 million by 2050.

With fertility below replacement level, even after its recent rise, only a small part of the expected increase in the British population will be the result of natural growth as people live longer. Life expectancy continues to rise at a rate that, until recently, no one anticipated – especially for men. Twenty-five years ago a 60-year-old British man could look forward to another 17 years of life, in 2006 he was looking at 21.[48] For women the equivalent figure was 21 years in 1984 and reached 24 by 2006.[49] Nevertheless, longevity is expected to account for just 15% of the nearly ten million increase in the population that the GAD expects over the next 25 years.

The rest will be either immigrants or their children. Without migration our population could be expected to rise to just 64 million by 2031, largely on the back of rising life expectancy, before starting slowly to decline.[50] It is hardly surprising, then, that immigration is the big story in British demography at the moment. To understand why, however, one needs first to examine what is happening with the native born population. In general, the British have been behaving in demographic terms very much in line with the rest of North West Europe. The total fertility rate has been hovering around 1.75 for 30 years. After dropping below

47 http://www.gad.gov.uk/Demography_Data/Population/index.asp?v=Table&pic=2006|uk|totpop

48 Government Actuary's Department, period cohort and expectations of life tables 2006; http://www.gad.gov.uk/Demography_Data/Life_Tables/Eoltable06.asp

49 ibid

50 Government Actuary's Department, 2006 population projections; http://www.gad.gov.uk/Demography_Data/Population/Index.asp?v=Principal&y=2006&subYear=Continue

1.7 at the beginning of this decade it has since recovered, and even managed to creep above 1.9 in 2007 (when a quarter of all babies had at least
one foreign born parent). As can be seen from the chart on page 5, recent
migrants have a higher level of fertility than those born in the UK – approximately two-and–a-half children for every woman compared to one-
and-three-quarters for those born in the UK.[51]

In absolute numbers, there were 690,013 births in 2007,[52] which was
substantially more than the Germans managed with nearly 20 million
more people, but fewer than the French with a roughly equal population.[53] But while overall fertility has held broadly steady over the last 30
years, both the mean age at which women first give birth and the percentage of babies born out of wedlock have risen dramatically. Thirty years
ago, less than 10% of children were born outside wedlock; in 2005, the
national figure was 43%.[54] Over the same period the number of babies
born to women aged 20-24 has more than halved, and for the last ten
years more women aged 30-34 have given birth than any other group.[55]

One common assumption that turns out to be incorrect is that as more
and more people are concentrated in the southern half of England, the rest
of Britain is gradually depopulating. During the 1990s, Scotland, Wales,
the North East and the North West did see a decrease in their populations, although it did not happen in all these regions every year. But the
biggest and most consistent loser by far over the last 30 years from *internal*
migration has, surprisingly, been London. Recently the exodus from the
capital has speeded up from 50-60,000 people a year to around 80,000.[56]
Meanwhile the biggest gainer from internal migration has not been, as
might be expected, the South East but the South West.

51 Office for National Statistics, news release, December 2007; http://www.statistics.gov.uk/pdfdir/fertil-
ity1207.pdf

52 Office for National Statistics, news release, July 2008; http://www.statistics.gov.uk/pdfdir/bdths0708.
pdf

53 Eurostat Live Birth Statistics; http://epp.eurostat.ec.europa.eu/tgm/table.do?tab=table&init=1&plugin=
1&language=en&pcode=tps00111

54 *Key Population and Vital Statistics*, No. 32, Office for National Statistics, 2005; http://www.statistics.
gov.uk/downloads/theme_population/KPVS32_2005/KPVS2005.pdf

55 *Population Trends 126*, Office for National Statistics, 2006

56 ibid

Internal migration, however, pales into insignificance besides its international counterpart. Throughout the '70s and '80s, the UK was a country of emigration. In the period 1980-85, the UN records an average net outflow of 50,000 per year. The picture today is entirely different. Even on the official figures, which many think underestimate the scale of recent immigration and which make no allowance for illegal arrivals, Britain has seen its population increase by over a million within just five years.

Net immigration into the UK has rocketed over the last decade, from around 60,000 a year in the '90s, to a peak of 255,000 in 2004-05. It should be stressed that these were net figures. Allowing for the 200,000 or so people who leave the country each year, the average number of arrivals has recently been running at nearly half a million annually. Never before have so many people come to live in this country in such a short time.

Put like that, it is understandable why people are nervous about immigration, especially as immigrants tend to settle in just a few urban areas. Between 1993 and 2002 over 700,000 immigrants came to live in London, more than making up for the number that left it over the same period.[57] And that was before immigration reached the high levels of the last few years. In London, foreign born residents now number around two million, or about a third of the population, and double the number of 20 years ago.[58]

The question many people want an answer to is how long will this go on – or, indeed, how long can it go on? The current official assumption is that future immigration will average 190,000 a year, for many years ahead. But the government has a poor record both when it comes to projecting population, and of keeping track of the numbers entering and leaving the country. In 1996, the last year the exercise was conducted under the Conservatives, the GAD thought net immigration would level off at 65,000 a year, and as late as 2002 its projection was 100,000. The Home Office also famously predicted that, at most, 13,000 East Europeans might arrive when their countries joined the EU in 2004.

57 *The Effect of Immigration on the Regions*, Migration Watch, 9th February 2005; http://www.migrationwatchuk.org/Briefingpapers/migration_trends/effect_of_immigration_onregions.asp
58 *Impact of Immigration on the London Economy*, LSE, July 2007

Today, no one knows for sure what the true number of recent arrivals from Eastern Europe is because, as EU citizens, registration is not compulsory. A total of 580,000 people from the eight former communist countries that joined the EU in 2004 had registered to work in the UK by the end of 2006.[59] Most observers, however, reckon the true number is much higher. By the start of 2007, 375,000 of those who had registered were Poles, but the Polish ambassador was reported as saying he thought nearer to 600,000 of his compatriots had arrived since May 2004[60]– although some of them are now returning.[61]

Equally striking is that immigration from elsewhere has also shot up in the last decade, not least from the Indian sub-continent. In the '80s and Nineties, primary immigration from the subcontinent virtually dried up, although admission for marriage and family reunion continued at the rate of around 25-30,000 a year. But after the millennium this changed dramatically. 50,000 people from India, Pakistan, Bangladesh, and Sri Lanka arrived in 2000, rising to 100,000 in 2006.[62] Part of this was due to an increase in the number of work permits issued, and part due to a large increase in the number of spouses and fiancés admitted, which doubled between 1996 and 2001.[63]

To work out what all this means for the future, the GAD, like the UN, produces projections based on a series of assumptions. Its principal projection shows the overall UK population rising by around 15% over the next 25 years, but within this there are wide differences between the growth rates for the various age groups. While the number aged under 55 is expected to remain roughly stable throughout the period, those aged 55-64 are expected to rise by 20%, the number of 65-84 year olds will grow by 50%, and the number of over-85s is set to quadruple.

As for how the population will be distributed, the chart shows the GAD's projections for the four constituent parts of the UK, with England

59 *The Daily Telegraph*, 28th February 2007

60 ibid

61 *The Times,* 16th February 2008; http://www.timesonline.co.uk/tol/news/uk/article3378877.ece

62 Office for National Statistics, news release, Emigration from UK reaches 400,000 in 2006, 15th November 2007; http://www.statistics.gov.uk/pdfdir/emig1107.pdf

63 *Immigration and Marriage,* Migration Watch, September 2004

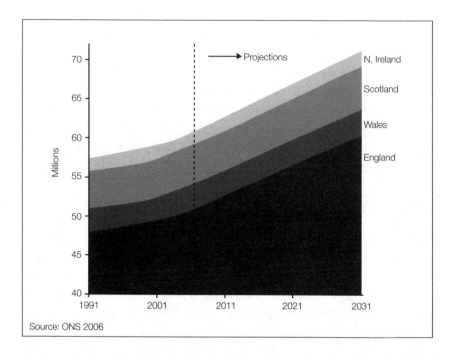

Source: ONS 2006

set to grow by 19% up to 2031 and Wales by 12%. Scotland, however, is expected to lose 8% of its population, while Northern Ireland is projected to grow by 5%.

However, it must be stressed, once again, that the GAD's current projections (and the UN's) do depend very heavily on the assumption that net immigration will continue at its current, very high level for decades to come. If it is wrong on this, and the reasons that it may be have already been touched on, then the British population in 20 years time – and especially the English part of it – will be significantly lower than it is forecasting, and the dependency ratio rather worse.

4: The Consequences

I grew up in Europe, where the history comes from.
Eddie Izzard

Very low fertility, populations that are ageing and shrinking, a looming collapse in the workforce, rapidly worsening dependency ratios and massive immigration, much of it illegal: on the face of it, the demographic outlook for Europe is grim. Whether Germany, Italy, Spain, the countries of Eastern Europe and the Baltic states will be able to turn their demography round over the next two decades is the big question for any study of the continent's population today. Even those who argue for smaller populations accept that to be sustainable such a shift would have to be gradual. The downward shift now confronting many European countries is imminent, and for some it is hard to see how it will be sustainable.

So is Pope Benedict right when he warns that Europe "seems to be following a path that could lead to its departure from History"? From a demographic point of view, three things need to be born in mind when considering the Pope's strictures. The first is the regional nature of what is happening, which has already been alluded to. For Britain and France, it will be a struggle to maintain our social security and healthcare systems and keep our finances and borders under control as our populations age. But these problems pale in comparison with the population-related difficulties facing the very low fertility countries of Southern, Central and Eastern Europe.

The second point is an economic one. So far Europeans have been able to take a relaxed view of their worsening demography only because the biggest economic challenge of all, the retirement of the baby boomers, is still ahead of us. Even this, however, is no longer far away. From 2010 onwards, those born immediately after the Second World War will start reaching 65. By 2015 – less than ten years away – the peak postwar cohort born in the '50s and early '60s will start retiring. It is only when this happens that the full economic impact of the continent's declining demography will start to be felt.

The third point is demographic, and one few people in Europe have yet taken on board although it could turn out to be the most important of all. It is that the UN Population Division forecasts for Europe – on which the previous chapter was based – are often at the optimistic end of the consensus. This book uses the UN forecasts because they offer the widest global coverage. As such, they form the best basis for comparing what is going on in Europe with the rest of the world. In one crucial respect, however, the UN is significantly more optimistic about Europe's prospects than most other experts.

In their latest projections the UN's demographers accepted that most of the very-low-fertility countries in South, Central and Eastern Europe are unlikely to meet their fertility assumption for the developed world of 1.85 children per woman by 2050. But the UN continues to aim on the high side; its latest assumption is that the TFR in countries such as Germany, Poland, Italy and Spain, will gradually recover to at or near 1.75 by mid-century. Even this, however, is noticeably more bullish than projections produced by the EU, the Council of Europe or most of the national governments concerned.

So, for instance, the UN has the TFR for Germany climbing from just over 1.3 today to 1.69 in 2050, and those for both Italy and Greece going from around 1.35 today to 1.75 by mid-century. But the comparable EU projections are 1.45 for Germany, 1.4 for Italy and 1.5 for Greece.[64] These differences may not sound much, but projected forward over the best part of half a century they would make a significant difference.

Perhaps the most intriguing (as well as ominous) question for our continent is what will society be like when these factors have played themselves out and we find ourselves living in a world that has twice as many pensioners as children? There will be plus points: an older society might well be more stable and there would probably be less crime. In political terms it would probably also be more conservative, if one considers that an advantage. But when fertility falls as low as it has in many European

64 *The Impact of Aging on Public Expenditure*, The Economic Policy Committee and the European Commission, 2006a; http://europa.eu.int/comm/economy_finance/publications/eespecialreports_en.htm

countries, the danger must be that the continent will find itself sucked into a downward demographic spiral of the sort the Pope fears.

In Vienna, the managing director of a big games company remarked: "The toy trade is slowly dying across central Europe. There are not enough children anymore." But it is not just toymakers who need to worry about the coming dearth of young people. Modern consumer culture revolves around youth; it, too, could find itself endangered. Design, the media, entertainment and advertising have always relied on young people for new ideas. Will fewer young people produce a nostalgic "Saga" culture? In Britain the number of over-80s has doubled to more than 2.5 million in 30 years and is expected to double again over the next 30. And we are comparatively youthful; in Italy there are already more octogenarians than toddlers under four.

None of this amounts to the imminent end of Europe, whatever the Pope may fear. But to overcome the demographic handicap that it will have to carry, Europe will have to run faster and faster if it is to do any better than just stand still.

Population Pyramid Selling

The first result to prosperity of a change over from an increasing to a decreasing population may be very disastrous.
Keynes

When numbers stagnate and then start to shrink the economic upheaval, as Keynes foresaw, could be severe. As the baby-boom generation moved through its working life in the late 20th century the proportion of the population at work rose while the proportion of those that were either retired or in education fell. This was Europe's "demographic window", and now it is about to close. Once the boomers start to retire, the fiscal sustainability of many European countries will come under enormous pressure, imperilling living standards for young and old alike.

Even before the credit crunch wreaked havoc with the continent's finances, the European Commission reckoned that the decline in the EU workforce could reduce its growth rate from an already niggardly 2% today to just over 1% by 2050.[65] So far, attention has focused on the strain an ageing society will put on pensions and healthcare. But pension and other welfare systems are not only affected by how long people live. The number in work is also crucial, because they are the ones who have to foot the bill. The relationship between the two is referred to as the old age dependency ratio, and if there are no longer enough young people to replace those retiring this ratio will deteriorate. In other words, as the bill gets bigger and bigger, the number of taxpaying workers to foot it will be getting smaller.

This is what is about to happen in Europe. In 1889, when Bismarck introduced the world's first state pension, German life expectancy was 48 and he set the pension age at 70, meaning that there were probably at least 100 workers to support each pensioner.[66] Now life expectancy in most developing countries is approaching 80, the pension age is often effectively around 60 due to early retirement (see Chapter 5), and in Germany there are just three workers to support each pensioner in its pay-as-you-go public retirement scheme. By 2035, it is expected that the ratio will have fallen still further, to below two workers per pensioner. It is a pattern that is set to be repeated, to a greater or lesser extent, right across Europe.

Up to now, most of the work that has been done on how to pay for an ageing society has been on what the costs are likely to be and how they can be contained. Very little thought has yet been given to the impact an older population will have on the tax base. But Europe's predominantly pay-as-you-go welfare model depends on a plentiful supply of tax. If a country's workforce, and perhaps even its overall economy, are shrinking, where is the money going to come from?

For decades now, the finances of most European governments have been based on what might be termed population pyramid selling. In the '60s and '70s, as the baby boomers entered the labour market governments were able to increase their tax take and big government took off. Something similar happened in other developed countries as well, but not to the same extent. Almost without exception, the percentage of

65 *Facing the Challenge, The Lisbon Strategy for Growth and Employment,* Report to the EU High Level Group, November 2004; http://ec.europa.eu/growthandjobs/pdf/kok_report_en.pdf
66 Ayres R, *The Economic Conundrum of an Ageing Population,* Word Watch Institute, September 2004

GDP taken by the state is higher in Europe than anywhere else – even anywhere else in the developed world.

Most people assume that Europe's high taxes date back to the aftermath of the Second World War. In fact, this is not so. Taxes did not rise, or at least not by very much compared with their prewar level, until much later. Research by the eminent Italian economist Vito Tanzi has established that at the start of the 1960s tax accounted on average for a little over 30% of GDP in most European countries – very much the same as just before the war.[67] The big tax hike actually occurred between 1960 and 1980. It was during those two decades, as the baby boomers entered the labour market, that European governments were able to raise their take to an average of 45% of GDP – roughly where it is today.[68]

The figures are surprisingly similar for all the major European countries. In France tax accounted for 29% of GDP in 1937 compared to just under 35% in 1960 and 48% in 1980. In Britain, the figures were 30% in 1937, 32% in 1960 and 43% in 1980. In Germany and Italy the tax take fell marginally between 1937 and 1960, but then rose to 42% and 48% respectively between 1960 and 1980.

The main reason for Europe's high tax is that in virtually all European countries pensions and healthcare are paid for largely out of current government receipts. As long as more workers were joining the labour force than leaving it, as they were in the 1970s and 1980s, such a model of social welfare was sustainable. But today the demographic dividend on which European governments relied when they raised tax in the 1970s and 1980s is starting to go into reverse, sharply so in the case of many countries.

The effect of the baby boomers' retirement on pensions has been much discussed, but has yet to be felt; 2020 will probably be the point at which pension schemes really start to feel the pinch of declining dependency ratios. Healthcare also gets more costly with age, and, with the number of those over 80 set to increase faster than any other group, the bill for sheltered accommodation looks sure to rise as well. The big question on all these items is how are we going to pay for them?

67 Tanzi V, *Death of an Illusion? Decline and Fall of High Tax Economies,* Politeia, September 2006
68 ibid

National governments invariably insist that their own pension and health systems are safe, even if their neighbours' might be a little dodgy. This is certainly the position of the British Treasury in its last report on the subject, *Long-Term Public Finance Report: an analysis of fiscal sustainability,* published in March 2008.

The paper produced estimates for spending on all the main areas of government right up to 2055, and also for what this would mean for taxes. It foresaw overall public expenditure rising by 4% of GDP by mid-century, with most of this conveniently occurring from 2030 onwards and all of it accounted for by pensions, health, long-term care and public service pensions. As far as tax is concerned the Treasury saw that rising by around 2%.

Put like this the future sounds if not exactly rosy, at least not too disturbing. The Treasury's own conclusion was that "the UK is well placed to deal with the fiscal consequences of population ageing."[69] But is this credible? After all, even before the current financial crisis public spending under Labour had risen by more than 4% in less than a decade, with minimal demographic pressure. To make its figures add up the Treasury report relied on two crucial assumptions, both of which also looked dubious even in better times. The first is that economic growth will average at least 2% a year for the next half-century. Yet most economists are agreed that, as countries age, growth is likely to slow. The second, equally bold assumption is that immigration will continue at its current, very high level right up to 2050. But this, too, looks far from assured.

The British Government, of course, is not alone in carrying out an optimistic exercise of this sort. Most European countries have made nervous calculations about their future finances, and most have come to similar, Panglossian conclusions. The European Commission has also devoted a lot of time to the issue; being more detached, its analysis tends to be more critical. In 2006 the commission published two large reports, one on ageing[70] and the other on future fiscal sustainability.[71] Launching the fiscal

---

69 *Long-Term Public Finance Report: an analysis of fiscal sustainability,* HM Treasury, 2008

70 *The Impact of Aging on Public Expenditure,* The Economic Policy Committee and the European Commission, 2006a; http://europa.eu.int/comm/economy_finance/publications/eespecialreports_en.htm,

71 *The Long-Term Sustainability of Public Finances in the European Union,* European Commission, http://ec.europa.eu/economy_finance/publications_en.htm, 2006b

sustainability report, the Economic and Monetary Affairs Commissioner, Joaquín Almunia, could hardly have been blunter. Surveying the prospects for Europe 50 years down the road, he warned:

> *Unless most Member States do something serious about defusing the pension time bomb, it will go off in the hands of our children and grandchildren, presenting them with a burden that is simply not sustainable. This is a problem that needs to be tackled through both a reduction of public deficits and debt and further reforms of the pension, health care and long-term care systems. Some progress has been made, but it is clearly not enough, and the window of opportunity during which the working-age population and overall employment levels will continue to rise, is closing fast.*[72]

To cope with the challenge, Mr Almunia told member states that they would have to do more than just get their budgets back into balance. If they were to have any hope of keeping their debt levels within manageable limits they would have to achieve a structural budget surplus of at least 2% a year, before their pension bills started to soar.[73]

Even in better days, this was a tall order. Since the 1980s most countries have massively increased their debts, and will continue to do so. In 2005 (the last year covered by the EU report) the four largest members, Germany, France, Britain and Italy, all ran a budget deficit of more than 3% of GDP. On overall national debt the position was a little better, with eleven members still within the Maastricht ceiling of 60% of GDP in 2005. Most of these, though, were new entrants from Eastern Europe. In "old" Europe the position was far worse, with the national debt of both Italy and Greece over 100% of GDP.

One could say, and many national finance ministers doubtless do in private, that it is easy for the EU to be frank on these difficult issues when it is the member governments that have to tackle them. But even Brussels fights shy of spelling out the implications of its strictures for living standards. The difficulty with reforming pensions is that it essentially means

72 ibid
73 ibid

either cutting them or raising the pension age, or some combination of the two. How, national politicians ask themselves, are they supposed to sell this to their ageing voters, when in many countries pensions are already low and getting lower?

Britain led the way in this field when it linked the state pension to prices rather than earnings over 20 years ago, and we are already backtracking. Faced with a growing problem of pensioner poverty, the Labour Government has introduced a supplementary pension credit, which is linked to earnings, and from 2011 the basic state pension is also to be relinked to earnings. In advance of the 2005 election Labour also backed down comprehensively on the thorny question of reforming public sector pensions.

Italy is also supposed to be reforming its notoriously generous pension system. But since the EU study was done it, too, has had to row back substantially on its planned reforms. In France, too, attempts at pension reform have had to be abandoned in the face of popular opposition. As for health and the provision of sheltered accommodation, very little has been done in any country to prepare for the strains an ageing society will inevitably impose on the budget for both these items.[74]

To a degree that is still largely unrecognised not just Europe's social model, but its whole idea of the role of government, depended on the buoyant demography of the baby boom. How the system can be adapted to cope when the demography goes into reverse, is something that no one has yet figured out – although many have tried.

The Clash of Generations

Will you still need me, / Will you still feed me, / When I'm 64?
The Beatles

It is not only the old who will feel the pinch as Europe ages. What makes the pension problem so intractable is that it is unfair on the young as well. In a speech on social security at Georgetown University, as long ago as

---

74 For a country by country analysis of prospective pension reform, see table on page 145

1998, Bill Clinton spelt this out to his student audience with a candour that few European politicians would dare to emulate:

> *If we don't do anything, one of two things will happen – either it will go broke and you won't ever get it; or if we wait too long to fix it, the burden on society of taking care of our generation's Social Security obligations will lower your income and lower your ability to take care of your children to a degree most of us who are your parents think would be horribly wrong and unfair to you and unfair to the future prospects of the United States.*[75]

Clinton was spot on in his analysis of the intra-generational tensions inherent in any modern welfare system when it is suddenly faced by a worsening dependency ratio. But at least public spending in the US has traditionally been comfortably below 40%, which even before the credit crunch was the case with only a handful of European countries. And in the US the numbers of working age are projected to continue to grow robustly right up to mid-century. If the US, with its comparatively buoyant demography, is going to have a problem how on earth will a shrunken working generation in Europe be able to afford both to raise their own children, and look after an ever increasing number of old people?

Any welfare or pension system rests on an implicit contract between the generations. For it to work, people of all ages must have a shared interest in its success. That used to be the case but it is not any more. It has been calculated that by 2020, two thirds of those aged over 60 in Germany, the most populous country in Europe, will have no grandchildren.[76] What incentive will they have to care about young people, and why should young people care about them? When different generations have such wildly divergent interests, any welfare system is liable to descend into a tug-of-war between the old and the young.

For those just starting their working lives, the outlook today is already much tougher than it was for their parents. In a series of reports, first published in 2005 and updated annually, the think tank Reform has dubbed

---

75 Clinton B speech; http://www.clintonfoundation.org/legacy/020998-speech-by-president-on-social-security.htm

76 *The Spectator*, 10th September 2005

British young people the "IPOD" generation: Insecure, Pressured, Over-taxed and Debt-ridden. This is how Reform saw the prospects for the IPOD generation in its first, 2005, report:

The balance of taxation and public spending has tilted against young people so that they now face an unfair burden. Key reasons for this change include:

- *An ageing population, forcing young people to support a much greater number of pensioners. The impact of this change will be felt in as little as five years from now.*

- *Unprecedented recent spending increases on the NHS, very largely used by older people.*

- *The introduction of tuition fees for higher education.*

- *The reduction in the real value of the basic state pension in the long term.*

- *Effective tax increases in regard to stamp duty and inheritance tax (which also make it more difficult for young people to share in rising housing equity).* [77]

In its 2007 report Reform reckoned that once student loan repayments are taken into account, the IPOD generation faced an effective combined tax rate of 49%. On top of that they also have to cope with house prices which, even after recent falls, have risen way beyond earnings since the turn of the decade. In Britain, according to David Willetts, the Conservatives' leading expert on social security, "We used to think of a society divided by class...but for today's children and young people there is another, still more significant division, that of age."[78] The date a person was born, Willetts suggests, is now one of the crucial determinants of how prosperous he can hope to be.

77 Bosanquet N and Gibbs B, *Class of 2005: The IPOD Generation*, Reform, 2005

78 Willetts D, "The Clash of Generations", a speech to Policy Exchange, 28th November 2005; http://policyexchange.moodia.co.za/Events/Past-Events.aspx?id=88

	Public Expenditure as % of GDP	Population aged 15-64 (thousands)			
EUROPE	2007	2005	2020	2035	2050
Austria	48.5	5 582	5 653	5 083	4 818
Czech Republic	43.6	7 244	6 852	6 662	5870
Denmark	50.8	3 581	3 518	3 328	3 334
Finland	47.3	3 496	3 360	3 225	3 172
France	52.4	39 725	40 020	39 024	38 468
Germany	43.9	55 063	52 036	43 165	38 739
Greece	43.3	7 485	7 388	6 825	6 024
Hungary	50.1	6 935	6 425	6 044	5 279
Iceland	43.1	196	244	248	236
Ireland	34.2	2 871	3 391	3 760	3 719
Italy	48.5	38 799	38 417	34 435	30 399
Luxembourg	38	313	375	407	458
Poland	42.6	26 897	25 187	23 319	18 354
Portugal	45.8	7 102	7 056	6 390	5 472
Slovak Republic	37.7	3 850	3 744	3 459	2 864
Spain	38.7	29 589	31 885	30 671	27 397
Sweden	52.6	5 934	5 993	6 101	6 280
UK	44.6	39 734	41 700	42 236	43 930
REST OF THE WORLD					
Australia	34.9	13 732	15 259	16 165	17 108
Brazil	19	123 339	147 084	147 795	137 166
China	27-30	924 229	996 036	950 580	870 115
India	27	704 611	916 278	1 061 287	1 097 969
Japan	36	84 487	74 022	64 444	51 790
Russia	38	101 828	91 895	82 294	70 086
United States	36.6	200 189	223 678	235 152	247 925

Source: UN World Population Prospects and Policy Exchange research

Across the Channel, the outlook is little better. The table on the previous page compares recent OECD data on levels of public spending across a range of countries with projections for the size of their future working populations. Although spending in most of them will have risen significantly since 2007, because of the global crisis, it still gives a good idea of which countries are most at risk from Europe's demographic time bomb. It could also be read as a useful guide to which offer the best and worst prospects for young people about to embark on their working lives.

The best long-term bet, despite its current woes, would seem to be Ireland, where public expenditure in 2007 was far below the European average and the working age population is projected to grow by over a quarter between 2005-2050. Britain, Sweden and France are in a middling group, where the outlook is for the working-age population to remain roughly stable or grow moderately over the next half century, but whose spending even in 2007 was already at a level which will make it hard to bear the extra costs of ageing.

Worst off of all will be ageing, shrinking countries that started out with a high tax burden and high level of public spending; in Germany, the number of people aged 15-64 is projected to fall by over 16 million, or 30% between 2004-2050, in Italy by more than eight million or 20% (despite its high immigration), and in Poland by eight million or 30%. In all these countries public spending was at least 45% of GDP, even before the credit crunch.

Reform's observation that "people under 35 could be described as a cross-over generation who are paying the cost of the welfare state without being able to expect many of its benefits" looks as true of the rest of Europe as it is of Britain. At one level, this is a matter of crude politics. Not only are the elderly becoming more prosperous and numerous, they are also more likely to vote – a combination which gives them formidable political clout.

In Britain, politicians of Gordon Brown's generation have tended to look at the young and asked how much tax they can pay not how much they can afford. Hence the proliferation of charges like stamp duty and tuition fees that hit them particularly hard. Partially on the back of these, Mr

Brown has lavished public money on pension credits and health services, both of which disproportionately benefit the elderly. Despite a real problem of pensioner poverty among the worst off, pensioners' incomes have more than doubled in real terms since 1979.[80] In America grey power has won a substantial rise in Medicaid. Meanwhile in both the US and Britain, where much of the pension system is privately run, today's workers are already having to pay increased contributions for what, in many cases, will turn out to be reduced benefits.

But while it may be an ageing world, this does not mean that the old can expect to have it all their own way for ever. The big decline in the ratio between workers and pensioners is still ten or more years away but, given the fiscal problems we are already facing, it is hard to see how the European social model can survive. The time must surely come when young people simply will not be able to afford to have the odds stacked ever higher against them. At the moment the system, both in America and Europe, is still run largely by the boomers. Only when that changes, as political leadership passes to the next generation, is it likely that the system may change as well.

The Power of Numbers

They say God is on the side of the big battalions.
Voltaire

Europeans may be shy of acknowledging it, but there is no denying that the rise of China and India makes us jumpy – and with good reason. In the past both these giants struggled to cope with their burgeoning populations. Now that they have joined the global economy they find that the power of numbers is on their side.

Some years ago Goldman Sachs caused a stir when it estimated that in less than 40 years time the economies of the so-called BRICs – Brazil, Russia, India and China – would be larger than the present G6.[81] Less than a decade

---

80 http://www.statistics.gov.uk/cci/nugget.asp?id=879

81 *Dreaming with the BRICs: The Path to 2050*, Global Economics Paper 99, Goldman Sachs, 2003; http://www2.goldmansachs.com/insight/research/reports/report6.html

later, we take as much for granted. The BRICs have been able to prosper not just because they have, on the whole, pursued hard-headed policies, but also because they are so large. With 2.75 billion people, the four BRICs account for 40% of the world's population.

Nor is it just the BRICs that Europe has to watch out for. In the 1980s the world trading system was largely confined to North America, Western Europe, Australasia, Japan, Taiwan and South Korea. Between them these countries boasted a population of well under a billion people. Now they have been joined not just by the BRICs, but the rest of the former Soviet bloc and much of Latin America. From a billion people 20 years ago, the globalised economy has expanded to cover at least four billion today.

Central to the economic prospects of most of these fast growing countries is that they are now entering their own demographic windows. Their economies are being boosted by growing populations in much the same way as the baby boom boosted European growth 40 years ago, only on an even bigger scale. Thanks to the opportunities opened up by globalisation, their labour forces have become their principal asset. Eventually these countries, too, will start ageing – in China's case surprisingly quickly. But in the meantime, provided they pursue a sensible course and the world economy does not completely collapse, countries with youthful and growing populations should be able to enjoy growth for a long time to come.

Not all of this is bad news for Europe. Over the last decade low cost imports have helped keep inflation down and this will continue. But the rise of the BRICs *et al* has also caused problems for the developed world, and all the signs are that these are increasing. For some time now, the high-cost countries of Western Europe and North America have had to accept losing manufacturing jobs to these new competitors. Britain, where the overwhelming majority of jobs are now in services, can claim to have adapted better than most. But the power of numbers can also be brought to bear on services. As developing countries become more sophisticated and their educational levels rise, we can expect more such jobs to follow their manufacturing predecessors to the low-cost, fast-growing economies of the East and Latin America. It will not just be call centres that are sent offshore; highly paid experts like software engineers and financial analysts will be equally vulnerable. One estimate, from a former deputy chairman of the Federal Reserve, Professor Alan Blinder, is that around 25% of all jobs in both Britain and the US could move abroad within the next 20 years.[82]

Estimates of skilled and unskilled workers (millions)

	Total		Unskilled		Skilled	
	2001	2030	2001	2030	2001	2030
World	3,077	4,144	2,674	3,545	403	598
High-income Countries	481	459	327	276	154	183
Other Countries	2,596	3,684	2,347	3,269	249	415
Of which China	773	870	740	816	33	54
Of which India	473	712	441	653	32	59

Source: World Bank Global Economic Prospects 2007

Nor will jobs be the only pinch point between the developed and developing worlds. Even if the world economy remains subdued for some time, we will increasingly have to compete with the BRICs as consumers of energy and raw materials. Here is what *The Economist* had to say in 2008 about China's burgeoning requirements:

> *There is no exaggerating China's hunger for commodities. The country accounts for about a fifth of the world's population yet it gobbles up more than half of the world's pork, half of its cement, a third of its steel and over a quarter of its aluminium. It is spending 35 times as much on imports of soya beans and crude oil as it did in 1929, and 23 times as much importing copper. Indeed, China has swallowed over four-fifths of the increase in the world's copper supply since 2000.[83]*

The force behind this ravenous demand is rapidly rising domestic consumption, a trend that has only just begun. After years of concentrating on exports, countries like China have been starting to treat themselves to a few of the comforts we in the West take for granted. China is already

82 *The Daily Telegraph*, 8th May 2007

83 *The Economist*, 15th March 2008

building the equivalent of Britain's entire electricity generating capacity every year, and by 2015 its car ownership is expected to treble. In 2005, in India, 200 Western-style shopping centres were on the drawing board, in 2000 there were just three.[84]

There are rapidly growing middle classes in many other countries as well, building themselves houses and buying themselves cars with just as much gusto as their counterparts in the BRICs. Goldman Sachs reckoned that, by 2015, 800 million people in the BRICs alone will be earning at least $3,000 a year – which it defines as the lower limit for a middle class standard of living. Eight hundred million new middle-class consumers is almost the same as the combined populations of the US, the EU and Japan. According to *The Economist,* in 1980 Asia's proportion of the global middle class was just 20%, in 2006 it had reached 60%.[85]

Whether or not all this will end in climate catastrophe, as many environmentalists argue, its effect has already been felt on the price of raw materials, and especially food and energy. It was rising demand from newly industrialising countries, with many more people consuming much more energy per head than they ever used to, that lifted the price of oil out of the $10-30 per barrel range in which it traded throughout the 1980s and 1990s. Before the global slowdown, China's oil consumption was rising at the rate of nearly 7% a year. Since most Indians and Chinese have yet to acquire cars, air-conditioners or even fridges, there is every reason to suppose that their need for energy will continue to grow for years to come. The International Energy Agency, which produces a comprehensive annual update on the world's energy prospects, expects China's oil imports to treble by 2030.

This helps to explain why, even though oil prices have now fallen back from their huge spike in summer 2008, they are still double the level they were right up until a few years ago. The same has also happened with food (see below), and even timber. Of course, raw material prices will always fluctuate according to the ups and downs of the global economy. But, in the longer term, as the world industrialises and its popu-

84 Brodsky S, "Married to the Mall", International Council of Shopping Centres, 2005; http://www.icsc.org/srch/sct/sct1105/feat_indiawed_married.php

85 *The Economist*, 12th February 2009

lation increases still further, we must expect the balance of economic power to continue to shift from the consumers of the world's resources to the producers.

The Military Equation

Less well understood is that demographic change will also have huge strategic and military implications for Europe – again, some good and some bad. Starting with the good: the days when European countries waged war on their neighbours are probably now truly over, if only because we no longer have enough young men to waste them on fighting each other. And while Russia may use its oil and gas to put pressure on its neighbours, even the most hard-line Kremlin adviser must know that it will struggle to revive as a great military power any time soon, given the near catastrophic loss in population that it faces.

Nor, as Europe gets older, will it have so much inclination to fight; in a senescent continent the focus of public spending will continue to shift away from defence and towards social services – as it has since the fall of the Berlin Wall. Only if a very direct military threat materialises are European countries likely to start spending again on guns rather than butter. But the other side of the coin is that Europe cannot expect to wield the clout and influence in the world that it has previously considered its right. Rather than being seen as either a rival or an ally, it is more likely to be seen as an irrelevance by both the US and the rising powers in the East. Already American commentators, particularly on the right, are wont to depict low-fertility Europe as being in terminal decline.

Meanwhile, America's own military and diplomatic muscle is being increasingly challenged by newly developing countries, their self-confidence boosted by their burgeoning populations and economies. But worrying though this is, at least countries like China and India are conventional powers and part of the established world order. Much more troubling is that the US and its allies have found it so difficult to deal with the low-tech opposition its forces have faced in Iraq and Afghanistan.

Demography has had a lot to do with this, too. For decades strategists have maintained that raw numbers should no longer be a decisive factor in military thinking. In an age of high tech warfare, professionalism, training and technology are supposed to be the keys to military success, not population. Yet in Iraq and Afghanistan none of this has helped anything like as much as the experts predicted. Even for a power as mighty and sophisticated as the US, occupying a third world country means putting boots on the ground – lots of them – and it has struggled to find enough. Ironically, Britain discovered this in relation to Iraq 90 years ago when we occupied the country in 1918, following the collapse of the Ottoman Empire at the end of the First World War. Iraq's population at the time was two million, compared with around 45 million for the United Kingdom. But even so we had to deploy more than 100,000 troops to hold the country in the face of tribal unrest and nationalist insurgency, and even with that many men we were hard pressed to keep control.

Since the 1920s populations across the Middle East have risen massively, but in terms of numbers the West still held the upper hand until well after the Second World War. In 1950 all the Arab countries put together had a population of just 60 million, compared with nearly 160 million in the US and a combined total of 120 million for Britain, France, and Spain – the three European powers which then still ruled territory in the Arab world.

By 2000 the demographic balance had changed dramatically. The Arab world had by then increased fourfold to just over 240 million, not far short of America's population. Over the same period the population of Iraq increased even faster, from under six million in 1950 to 25 million in 2000 – and approaching 30 million today. In Afghanistan (which is not an Arab country) it went up at a similar pace, from eight million to 20 million by 2000, and approaching 30 million today.

Thanks to their high fertility, these countries are also now much younger then the West. Between 1950 and 2000, America's average age rose from 30 to 35, and in Europe it went from 30 to nearly 38. In Iraq and Afghanistan the average age fell over the same period; in Iraq it was just 18 in 2000 and 16 in Afghanistan. The result, as America and Britain have discovered to their cost, is that both countries have disproportionately large reserves of fighting age men.

In a region which is already unstable, fast growing, young and largely unemployed populations are highly likely to spell trouble, even if Western nations steer clear of them. Professor Samuel P Huntington, author of the seminal *The Clash of Civilizations*, links the instability of the Middle East directly to the frustration of its large number of unemployed but relatively educated youth. Many oil producers, Huntington points out, have used their newfound wealth to educate their people, but few, if any, have fostered sufficient economic growth to employ them.[86]

Across the Middle East, youth unemployment was estimated by the International Labour Organisation at 25% in 2003, the highest in the world. As the populations of these countries grow so, too, do the number of unemployed, by at least 500,000 a year according to the ILO.[87] As elsewhere in the developing world, more and more of them are concentrated in the slums of large cities. Within ten years over 70% of the region's population will be urban, with a quarter living in cities of one million or more.[88] For any potential invader demography like this is a nightmare.

Just how much of a nightmare was the subject of a seminal article in 1995 entitled "Force Requirements in Stability Operations" by James T Quinlivan, an analyst at the Rand Corporation and leading authority on the subject. In his article Quinlivan pointed out that "the populations of countries in the underdeveloped world have expanded markedly relative to the population of the United States. More particularly, the populations of Third World countries have expanded even more dramatically relative to the size of the American military."[89]

Quinlivan's conclusion was that "first, very few states have populations so small that they could be stabilized with modest-sized forces. Second, a number of states have populations so large that they are simply not candidates for stabilization by external forces."[90] Quinlivan also looked at how many peacekeepers had been required for counter-insurgency campaigns since the Second World War, and found that while some had only required as few as four per 1,000 inhabitants, more difficult campaigns like

86 Huntington S, *The Clash of Civilisations and Remaking of World Order*, Free Press, 2002

87 International; Labour Organisation, Key Indicators of the Labour Market, 2007; http://www.ilo.org/public/english/employment/strat/kilm/download/kilm09.pdf

88 UN, World Urbanization Prospects, 2007 revision, figures given for Western Asia; http://esa.un.org/unup/p2k0data.asp+

89 Quinlivan J, "Force Requirements in Stability Operations", *Parameters*, Winter 1995, pp 59-69; http://www.carlisle.army.mil/usawc/Parameters/1995/quinliv.htm

90 ibid

the British ones in Malaya and Northern Ireland have needed up to 20 per 1,000 inhabitants.

On this analysis, at 20 peacekeepers per 1,000 inhabitants for a tough operation, America should have deployed 500,000 troops in Iraq, compared to the 150,000 or so who have struggled to maintain an uneasy peace since the fall of Saddam. On the same basis, Nato would also have to find half a million personnel to deal with Afghanistan. Yet neither Afghanistan nor Iraq is an especially large country by the standards of today's developing world. Iran and Pakistan, both countries in which the US could yet find itself embroiled, are far more populous. What goes for Middle Eastern demography is also true of Africa. In 1950 the countries that now comprise the EU had a combined population one and a half times that of Africa. Now Africa outnumbers the EU by more than two to one, and by 2050 the ratio is expected to be five to one.

Many Western leaders, though, still appear to think they can hold sway over both regions, much as they did 50 or a hundred years ago. Clearly Europe is going to have to continue to take an active interest in both the Middle East and Africa. But we also need to realise that, when it comes to war, demography once again matters.

One of the most important lessons of Iraq is that, in our future dealings with both these unstable regions, the power of numbers is going to be on their side not ours.

The Human Stain

> If I were a Brazilian without land or money or the means to feed my children, I would be burning the rain forest too.
> Sting

Environmentalists tend to think that more people must always mean more mess and the next 50 years will probably prove them right. In Britain, the

Optimum Population Trust has campaigned for years for a shrinking population. Its latest suggestion is that we should aim for a reduction in the order of
50%.[91] That would be extreme, but the question of how large a population
the world can sustain has been worrying people ever since Malthus's day.

In Europe population growth will end very soon, but any environmental benefits are likely to be more than offset both by the increase in numbers in the rest of the world, and also by the rapid rise in energy use and
pollution in newly developing countries. If the whole world's population
begins to fall by mid-century, as expected, these factors, too, should tail
off. In the meantime, however, concern about the availability of energy,
water and food is growing in the face of soaring global demand.

Climate change is beyond the remit of this book, but the pressure
on natural resources, pollution and global warming are really all aspects
of a single, even larger question: will the world be able to sustain a
population of nine billion or more by mid-century? The good news is
that from now on the pace of population growth, while still enormous,
should be slowing down. Over the next 25 years the global population
is projected to increase by slightly less than it did over the last 25 years
(see p50), and although pollution increased dramatically over that period, in most other ways the world coped surprisingly easily. Worldwide
food production per capita, for instance, actually rose and the incidence
of famine and hunger fell.[92]

The bad news is that none of this can be taken as a reliable guide to the
future. The huge rise in the world's population that occurred over the last
quarter of a century was concentrated overwhelmingly in poor countries.
And for most of that period, most of those countries stayed poor. In some
cases, mostly in Africa, they even got poorer. Only latterly did some of
them, mainly in Asia, begin to develop on any appreciable scale. So while
the demand placed on the world's resources by population growth in the
second half of the last century was real enough, it was limited by the poverty of the countries where it occurred.

91 Based on its assumption that our ecologically sustainable population is currently between 17 and 27
million, less than half of our total population, OPT news release, February 2008; http://www.optimum-
population.org/opt.release18Feb08

92 Global Hunger Index, International Food Policy Research Institute, 2008

It is this that is now changing. Much of the growth in numbers over the next half century will again be in Africa, and unfortunately there is little likelihood that living standards in most African countries will start rising quickly any time soon. But elsewhere, countries that have recently begun to develop rapidly will also see massive population increases. For the environment, this double whammy of fast growing populations coupled with rapid economic growth in countries where it was previously minimal, represents a huge and new challenge. We have not seen the like of today's combination of fast growing populations and fast growing economies since the late 19th century. Because of it the pressure on all natural resources is increasing far more rapidly than anyone thought possible just a few years ago. So, inevitably, are the pollution, environmental exhaustion and carbon emissions that these fast growing, fast industrialising populations produce.

Few experts until very recently doubted that the world would be able to feed the extra mouths that are expected over the next half century. The general view was that, provided agricultural productivity continued to increase at around the same rate as it has over the last four decades, food supplies should not be a problem. Over the last year or two, however, it has become clear that this benign scenario rests on assumptions which may no longer be valid. For a start, it assumes that agricultural productivity can continue to improve. Given problems over water supplies and political controversy over new agricultural technologies such as genetically modified crops, this can no longer be taken for granted. Secondly, it assumes that eating habits remain largely unchanged. Only very recently has anyone begun to factor in that as people in previously poor, undeveloped countries get richer their diets are likely to become more sophisticated.

As demand increases in one area, so it creates extra pressure in others. The consumption of milk and meat, for instance, has soared in many Asian countries over the last 15 years and supplying both is far more resource intensive than growing rice. It requires large amounts of water, when water supplies in many places are already under pressure. It also requires fuel, especially as much of the new Asian demand for both meat and milk has been met by imports. Meanwhile the demand for biofuels to replace oil has also grown, especially in the United States, and land

and water that is used for biofuel cannot also be used to produce food. A report in 2007 from Credit Suisse estimated that world food production will need to grow at 3.3% a year to satisfy demand from changing dietary needs and the biofuel market.[93] It broke the overall figure down as 1.1% to cope with population growth, 0.8% because we are eating more, 0.6% for more expensive diets, and 0.8% for biofuel.[94]

What goes for diet goes for lots of other things as well. Not only will there be more people to feed, clothe and shelter in places like India, Brazil, Mexico and China, but as they get richer their per capita consumption will also rise. Will we be able to cope or could all those Malthusian warnings over the years that the Earth's resources are finite be about to be proved right? Could we even run short of food in prosperous Europe? It seems inconceivable but after 50 years in which virtually no one in the developed world has had to worry about the availability of food (or even its price), some experts are beginning to think that we may be in for a shock.

Professor Bill McKelvey, chief executive of the Scottish Agricultural College, caused something of a stir when he warned in 2007: "In the UK we are becoming less self-sufficient in food. I think it's possible in the next 25-50 years that there will be shortages of food in the UK." He also cautioned that the proportion of average family income spent on food might double from 10 to 20%. According to a report prepared in April 2009 for the agricultural ministers of the G8, for people in the developing world, it will not only be a matter of the price of food going up but whether enough will be available to go around at any price. To avoid widespread hunger, the report predicted, food production would have to double by 2050 to deal with the combination of bigger populations, rising prosperity and climate change.

Water will be another worry. It may fall from the skies, but anyone who lives in the South of England knows that it is getting harder to meet our ever-increasing requirement for fresh supplies. Any visitor to Cairo or Mexico City will have seen how shanty towns are spreading unchecked around the developing world, and the enormous pressure on clean water supplies this

93 "Higher Agricultural Prices Opportunities and Risk", Credit Suisse, 6th November 2007
94 ibid

causes. The UN calculates that 700 million people live in areas of what it terms water scarcity. It expects this to increase to three billion by 2025[95] – many of them in large cities, and some in developed regions like the American South West.[96] A 2008 report from the OECD classed South East England as among the regions in the world at highest risk of severe droughts over the next half-century, unless more is done to constrain demand.[97]

All these problems come back to the question of whether the world's carrying capacity will be able to cope with the double whammy of rapid demographic and economic growth at the same time. To do so, we will have to find new sources of energy and raw materials, squeeze more out of current resources, and use less of them. Higher prices should eventually force us to make these adjustments whether we want to or not, and also help to make new technologies economic. A high price for oil, economically difficult though it may be, will be crucial in encouraging both efficiency and new alternative forms of supply. But this will not necessarily make the environmentalists happy. Professor McKelvey believes the only way to solve world food shortages is for farming to become more, not less, intensive:

> The bottom line is that food security is not a given. Farmers need to increase production, and in this context organic production is very much a niche... Modern agriculture has provided us with cheap, plentiful food. It will need to be even more efficient if it is to meet the world's needs for food and energy.[98]

More use of nuclear power will not be popular with environmentalists either, but again few experts doubt that it will be necessary if the West is to keep the lights on over the next 50 years, whatever the advances in alternative renewable sources.

95 UN Secretary-General, statement for World Water Day, 12th March 2007; http://www.un.org/News/Press/docs/2007/sgsm10906.doc.htm

96 UN Secretary-General, address to World Economic Forum, 24th January 2008; http://www.un.org/News/Press/docs/2008/sgsm11388.doc.htm

97 The Daily Telegraph, 5th March 2008; http://www.telegraph.co.uk/earth/main.jhtml?xml=/earth/2008/03/05/eaoecd105.xml

98 The Guardian, 18th April 2007; http://www.guardian.co.uk/commentisfree/2007/apr/18/foodforthought

The one thing that seems most unlikely to have much effect on consumer behaviour is exhortation, particularly if it is the West exhorting the rest of the world to save the planet by foregoing the comforts and pleasures we take for granted. The silver lining, if there is one, is that higher prices and shortages mean that, as population continues to expand, we will have no choice but to adopt a more sparing and respectful approach to the world's natural bounty.

5: Can we do anything about it?

Fate can be taken by the horns, like a goat, and pushed in the right direction.
American Proverb

There is nothing we can do to stop the populations of China, India, Brazil or the US growing faster than Europe's will over the next 30 years. For better or worse, all countries will feel the impact of the huge global shifts that population change will unleash. As others pull ahead, Europe's relative importance is bound to decline and the competitive pressures on us will inevitably increase. Much more could be done, however, to mitigate the impact of population change on Europe, but only if politicians and policymakers show more willingness to face up to it than they have to date.

The economy may be slumping at the moment, but further down the line no one doubts that European countries, including Britain, face a problem of labour supply. The workforce is falling, often outright or (as in our case) relative to the overall population. It is a scenario which does not give us many choices: either we will have to rely on immigration or we are going to have to find extra sources of labour domestically.

Immigration is always a hot topic and over the last decade it has become even hotter as the pace of arrivals has speeded up, both here and in other European countries. Governments invariably tell their voters that they are determined to control immigration, by which they usually mean reduce it. But contrary to the way they are often portrayed, immigrants tend to go where they think they are wanted or, at any rate, needed. If we really intend to limit immigration then reducing the demand for it will be crucial. This, in turn, will only be possible if we can make better use of the indigenous workforce.

It is not that anyone really doubts the need to improve Europe's chronically inefficient labour markets. The problem is that doing so will present enormous political difficulties. Later retirement is the most obvious expedient, but it is rarely popular. Even during the recent good times a large number of working-age people in many European countries, including Britain, were not working but living on benefits. In theory it should be possible to cajole a good proportion of them back into the labour force. In practice, we already know that this will not be easy. A third approach, increasing the proportion of women in work – the so-called female participation rate – is the object of deep suspicion in many socially conservative countries. As politicians are only too aware, not only would measures like these take time to make an impact but they would often be even more unpopular than immigration. To quote Frits Bolkestein: "Pay more, work longer and get less, is not an easy message to sell."

In the longer term an even bigger question, especially, for those countries facing outright falls in their populations is what, if anything, can be done to boost Europe's flagging birth rates. Political leaders have a bad track record when it comes to trying to dictate the pace of procreation. In Europe, where attempts to increase fertility have often been associated with dictatorship, they are especially nervous of doing so. It is hard to imagine any European politician exhorting families, as the Australian Treasurer Peter Costello did, to "have one for mum, one for dad, and one for the country."[99]

Yet despite this, there are strong reasons for supposing that, in nearly all European countries, women now consistently have fewer children than they originally wanted – or, at least, say they wanted. Surveys regularly show that most European women would like to have at least two children, but as they put off having their first baby to an ever later age, so the chances of them having a second recede. In countries where this becomes the norm the risk is that one child families will also become the norm, and many more women than previously will have no children at all. Today, in Germany, a third of 40-year-old women do not have children.[100] Once trends like this become established and accepted, they become very hard to reverse.

This "baby gap" or "baby hunger" is the counterpart of Europe's baby famine, but although it lies at the heart of the continent's demo-

---

99 BBC News, 2nd June 2006; http://news.bbc.co.uk/1/hi/world/asia-pacific/5040582.stm
100 Deutsche Welle, 2005; http://www.dw-world.de/dw/article/0,2144,1705794,00.html

graphic problems it is rarely addressed by politicians or policymakers – or even pundits.

Immigration

> *Bring me your huddled masses.*
> Inscription on the Statue of Liberty, New York

Large scale immigration into Europe began after the Second World War, when Britain and France began to receive migrants from their former colonies, and a large number of Turks moved to Germany as guestworkers. In the 1970s growth slowed, and by the 1980s Europe had again become self-sufficient in labour thanks to the postwar baby boom. Together with the introduction of tougher controls and the recurrent economic crises of the '70s and '80s, this led to a drop in immigration that lasted for the best part of two decades.

Recently immigration has been on the rise again, and in many countries it is back at the top of the political worry list. For the current Labour government, which all along has wildly underestimated the scale of British immigration, the subject is certainly a sore one. Labour has been widely criticised not just for relaxing many of the old controls, but for failing to foresee the consequences.

To be fair to Labour, it was not alone in failing to read the runes on immigration correctly. Other European countries also sucked in large numbers of immigrants, often unwittingly, and are now unhappy about it. While approximately 9% of people in the UK were born elsewhere, for France and Germany the figures are 11% and 12.5% respectively.[101] Nor was Labour alone in failing to anticipate the huge influx of East Europeans after May 2004 – which, it should also be remembered, was widely welcomed at first.

Where Labour really went wrong on immigration was that, all too often, ministers saw it as a quick fix to deal with deep-seated demographic and economic problems. In particular, they failed to understand

101 Migration Policy Institute, citing OECD database, 2005; http://migrationinformation.org/charts/pop-table2-jun06.cfm

that, when it comes to trying to maintain the labour supply immigration, pension reforms and labour market reforms are all aspects of the same problem, and all of them will have to be part of the solution.

In demographic terms, the notion that immigration can be used to offset the impact of a declining indigenous population on a country's dependency ratio can be fairly easily dismissed. Because immigrants themselves grow old, and also because the birth rates of immigrant communities tends to fall to that of their host country, "replacement migration" would require an endless and increasing stream of arrivals just to keep the situation steady.

In 2000 the UN calculated how many immigrants each country in the then EU 15 would need to attract by 2050 to maintain the current dependency ratio between workers and pensioners, assuming its birth rate remained at current levels. The numbers it came up with were staggering. Germany alone would need 188 million migrants by mid-century, or over three-and-a-half million a year, and Italy 120 million. To put that in context, Italy, which already has the second highest level of immigration in Europe at over 300,000 a year, would have to increase that *eightfold* to keep its dependency ratios at 2000 levels. Britain, which has a birth rate above the European norm, would need just under 60 million immigrants by 2050. That would work out at just under 1.2 million new arrivals a year, every year. By 2050 the British population would double to 120 million.[102]

Unsurprisingly, these findings caused huge political embarrassment, even though the intention was to demonstrate the impracticality of replacement migration rather than advocate it. When the fuss died down, the EU is said to have quietly insisted that the exercise should never be repeated. But what about the more immediate issues raised by immigration? Social cohesion apart, debate on the subject really revolves around three questions. The first is how beneficial is it, and can we draw up a balance sheet of the costs and benefits? The second is to what degree can we, in fact, control it? The third question, assuming that we can exercise control, is how many migrants should we aim to take? Only in the last few years,

102 UN Population Division, 2000

after a decade in office, has Labour really begun to address any of these difficult and delicate issues, or consider their long-term consequences.

Of the three, the first question is the simplest to answer. Like it or not, no one can deny the huge role immigrants now play in our economy and society, or in those of other large European countries. Even in today's more austere economy industries like hospitality, construction and fruit farming would be lost without foreign workers. Over half of all newly qualified nurses are foreign born.[103] Immigrants also run most small convenience shops, many thousands of restaurants and a host of other small businesses, which add greatly to both our economy and our culture.

In London, where the foreign population has doubled from one to two million in 20 years, the impact has been even more marked. A recent study by the LSE found that immigrants make up 60% of the workforce in the capital's hotels and restaurants, and a similar proportion in domestic service. In the highly paid financial services sector they accounted for 25% of all jobs, and in both education and public administration for 20%.[104] Clearly, immigration has brought many benefits and trying to do without it would be very difficult indeed.

Just because we have come to rely on it, however, does not make it an economic panacea. Putting together a balance sheet for immigration is notoriously hard. A Home Office study published in 2002 suggested that in 1999-2000 immigrants contributed £2.5 billion more in taxes than they cost in public spending.[105] However, the figure was vigorously and convincingly disputed by a number of economists. The conclusion at the end of a pretty robust argument was that, in fiscal terms, the impact of immigration in Britain has probably been roughly neutral in recent years.

Trying to estimate immigration's effect on overall economic growth has proved equally difficult, and equally contentious. The Government has produced various figures for the extra output that it claims can be attributed to immigration. But when the House of Lords Select Com-

103 *Success with Internationally Recruited Nurses*, Royal College of Nursing, 2005

104 *The Impact of Immigration on the London Economy*, London School of Economics, 2007

105 Gott C and Johnston K, *The Migrant Population in the UK: fiscal effects*, Home Office Research, Development and Statistics Directorate in collaboration with the Performance and Innovation Unit of the Institute of Public Policy Research, RDS Occasional Paper No 77, February 2002; www.homeoffice.gov.uk/rds/pdfs/occ77migrant.pdf

mittee on Economic Affairs examined the issue in 2008 it concluded that the Government had been addressing the wrong question. According to the Committee:

> *Overall GDP, which the Government has persistently emphasised, is an irrelevant and misleading criterion for assessing the economic impacts of immigration on the UK. The total size of an economy is not an index of prosperity. The focus of analysis should rather be on the effects of immigration on income per head of the resident population. Both theory and the available empirical evidence indicate that these effects are small, especially in the long run when the economy fully adjusts to the increased supply of labour. In the long run, the main economic effect of immigration is to enlarge the economy, with relatively small costs and benefits for the incomes of the resident population.[106]*

The committee is surely right that what matters is GDP per capita, but this, too, is only part of the story. While the impact of immigration may have been neutral in overall terms it has also been distinctly uneven.

Cheap imported goods are something everyone can benefit from. But importing people impacts on the home-grown population in very different ways, depending on how rich you are, where you live and a whole range of other factors. Migration Watch, as its name suggests, is a think tank which specialises in immigration. It makes no bones about its opposition to mass immigration, but its work is respected on all sides because its figures and analysis have generally proved far more accurate than the Government's. It has made a series of studies of the impact of large-scale immigration in Britain, including on housing, services and employment, the findings of which are revealing.

Take wages and employment. For employers the advantages of a ready supply of cheap skilled labour are obvious. Polish plumbers, Czech nannies and Slovakian waitresses were all greeted with open arms when they first arrived because their skills were in short supply among the home-grown labour force. The same goes for Bangladeshi cooks in Indian res-

---

106 House of Lords, Select Committee on Economic Affairs, *The Economic Impact of Immigration, vol 1*, 2008; http://www.publications.parliament.uk/pa/ld200708/ldselect/ldeconaf/82/82.pdf

taurants and Filipino nurses. If we had not had so many immigrants over the last few years, there is little doubt that the economy would have been less efficient and wage inflation higher.

From an employer's point of view, this makes immigration an obviously good thing. But if you are an unskilled indigenous worker at the bottom of the income scale, who is liable to be priced out of an already low paid job by a cheaper migrant, it can be a very bad thing. The London study by the LSE, cited above, found that:

> *There must … be at the least a very strong suspicion that the real wages of those working in the worst paid set of jobs in London have been substantially reduced as a consequence of the influx of new migrants, many of who, though formally qualified for better jobs, have been unable to access them.*[107]

Findings like these help to explain the paradox, also seen in other European countries, that it is possible to attract large numbers of immigrants even when large number of home-grown workers are out of work.

Housing and public services are two other areas where the impact of immigration is good for some but not for others. Britain, and especially England where most immigrants settle, has traditionally had tighter controls on house building than any other comparable nation. America has five times our population, but it was building between ten and twelve times as many new homes a year before the sub-prime mortgage crisis struck. France, with the same size population and lower immigration, has recently been building twice as many new homes each year. Spain, which has a population two-thirds the size of ours, was building homes at three times our rate before its market crashed.[108]

In Britain, by contrast, even in the good times we were barely building enough new houses and flats to meet home-grown demand. With supply so constrained, immigration can only push the already high price of housing even higher. In relation to London, the LSE study found

107 *The Impact of Immigration on the London Economy*, London School of Economics, 2007
108 Housing Statistics in the EU, 2004

that: "The increase in demand for housing generated by immigrants increases both house prices and the incentive to increase supply. Supply, however, is relatively inelastic – so it is the impact on prices which dominates." On the national level Migration Watch has calculated that net immigration of 140,000 a year would require the provision of over 60,000 extra homes a year, or 250 a day in England alone, just to keep up with the new arrivals.[109] Net immigration of 190,000, which is the current official assumption, would push that closer to 80,000 a year.

For existing home owners keeping an anxious eye on property values this may be a boon, but for those struggling to get on the housing ladder, competition from immigrants is less welcome. It is much the same with education and health. If you live in a poor area where large numbers of immigrants have suddenly arrived, your schools and surgeries will be under pressure. But if you can afford to live in a leafy suburb or go private, you will probably gain from the easy availability of foreign doctors and nurses.

That immigration tends to be good for the well off, but much less so for those at the bottom of the scale, is now generally accepted. If it were to be stopped, or even substantially curtailed, the middle classes and a lot of industries would lose out. But not everyone would be a loser, and the low paid and unskilled might well gain.

What about the second question, can we control immigration? In one sense this is less controversial than the first, because virtually everyone now agrees that control must be exercised. It is just that often it seems impossible to achieve. In most countries, some categories can come virtually as of right, usually for marriage or family reasons. In Britain, the number of fiancés and spouses admitted annually has doubled since 1996 (see p61). Others arrive as students; in theory they should go home when their courses are over but in practice many stay. Both these categories would be hard to reduce; students because of the impact on universities, family arrivals for legal and human rights reasons. In addition, no control at all is possible on EU citizens (except Bulgarians and Romanians until 2014) even if they were originally immigrants to another EU member state.

109 *The Impact on Housing of Immigration in England,* Migration Watch UK, 2007

Nevertheless, while these categories are significant, many immigrants do not arrive as of right but either with permission or illegally. Demographers call the factors that attract migrants to one country rather than another, "pull" factors. These are usually things like benefits and jobs over which receiving countries can exert at least some control. But the situation in the countries that the immigrants leave is also important, indeed often more so. Very often, of course, the reason is poverty or insecurity. These and other "push" factors are just as significant in determining migration, as anything that receiving countries say or do.

Crucially, these push factors include not just the economic and political situation in migrants' home countries, but also their demographic outlook. For Britain, which has become so dependent on East European immigrants in recent years, it is particularly important to realise that such factors can push immigration down as well as up. The Poles and other young East Europeans who have flocked to Western Europe over the last few years came largely because wages at home were low and jobs scarce.

But in Eastern Europe the demographic outlook is even more challenging than it is in Western Europe. In all these countries, the current 15-24 age group were the last generation mainly to be born before the collapse of communism, and with it the collapse of East European birth rates. As the impact of lower, post-communist fertility works through, numbers in this age group will soon start to drop dramatically. In Poland and Romania (the two biggest countries in the region) the number of 15-24s is set to fall by 30% between 2005 and 2015, in the Czech Republic by 22% and in Hungary by 15%. Far from having an endless surplus of young people to export, these countries will soon be facing demographic shortfalls of their own. For this reason, alone, it is likely that the outflow of young people from Eastern Europe will end quite soon. Indeed, it may already have done so.

Meanwhile in Africa and the Middle East not only is there an enormous supply of potential migrants waiting to come, but in some countries it is about to get very much bigger. In Africa 20% of the population is aged 15-24 – a total of 190 million young people in 2005. By 2015 that will rise to nearly 230 million and by 2025 to around 280 million. In the Middle East the number of young people is projected to rise more slowly from around 40 to 45 million between 2005 and 2015.

With few prospects at home, large numbers from both these poor and troubled regions will continue to be drawn to Europe – whether we want them or not. According to the International Labour Organization (ILO), in 2005 there were eight-and-a-half million unemployed people aged 15-24 in the Middle East and North Africa, and twice that many in sub-Saharan Africa. And among those who were employed nearly ten million in the Middle East and North Africa, and 70 million in sub-Saharan Africa were earning under $2 a day. Add just some of these figures together and it comes to an awful lot of potential migrants for whom Europe is the obvious destination.[110]

At a seminar in June 2006, Rear Admiral Chris Parry, head of the developments, concepts and doctrine centre at the Ministry of Defence, warned what these pressures could mean over the next 30 years.[111] Parry cautioned that war or disaster in the third world could unleash a wave of mass migration directed at Europe and widespread piracy in the Mediterranean which would directly threaten the shores of Southern Europe. "At some time in the next ten years," he warned, "it may not be safe to sail a yacht between Gibraltar and Malta."[112] The Rear Admiral's language was unusually vivid, but mass illegal immigration from the Middle East and Africa is already a fact, and it is growing rapidly.

In October 2005 the twin Spanish enclaves of Ceuta and Melilla, perched precariously on Morocco's Mediterranean coast, had a dramatic foretaste of what Parry was talking about. As the only fragments of EU territory in Africa, both towns have long been magnets for would-be illegal immigrants. But in autumn 2005 they faced something far more dangerous. They found themselves, quite literally, under siege, not by Morocco (whose claims to the territories Madrid has long ignored) but by tens of thousands of Africans desperate to break into Europe.

What made the whole episode even more unnerving was that few of the invaders were North African. Mainly they were West Africans who had trekked on foot for months on end, across the Sahara, in the hope of somehow, anyhow reaching Spain. At the height of the crisis, the Euro-

110 http://www.ilo.org/public/english/region/ampro/cinterfor/temas/youth/doc/youth_en.pdf
111 *Sunday Times*, 11th June 2006
112 ibid

pean Commission said it had intelligence reports of 30,000 West Africans travelling through Morocco and neighbouring Algeria en route to the enclaves, many from as far away as Mali and Niger.[113]

Within months, the Spanish were facing a new onslaught, this time in the Canary Islands. 30,000 were caught trying to enter there in 2006, having made the journey in overcrowded open boats from Mauritania or Senegal.[114] In Italy, in the same year, 21,000 would-be illegal immigrants were caught arriving by boat, often having set out from Libya.[115] Even tiny Malta intercepted nearly 2,000 Africans trying to get to Europe.[116] For every one that was caught, probably at least one other will have entered undetected. Many more will have perished in appalling circumstances at sea.

Faced with pressures like this, it is not surprising that it is getting harder and harder to reduce illegal immigration. Obviously, improving controls and patrols is important and both the EU and individual countries are now doing this. But even most illegal migrants do not up sticks and risk all on a perilous journey to a country of which they probably know very little, unless they think they will find work at the end of their quest. Just across the Mediterranean from the poverty of Africa and the Middle East lie Italy, Greece and Spain. All of them have long coast lines that are very difficult to police, all of them are ageing rapidly and all of them are bedevilled by chronically inefficient labour markets. No wonder the immigrants keep coming when they know that if they can only get in to these countries, their low-paid services will be in demand.

And once they have a toehold in Europe there is little to stop them moving on, eventually even to Britain. All of which means that if we are serious about limiting immigration then we will have to accept that visas, border controls etc, while all very important, are only going to be part of the answer. Demand will also have to be reduced, which is where the third question comes in: how many migrants should we be aiming to take?

---

113 BBC News, 14th October 2005; http://news.bbc.co.uk/1/hi/world/africa/4343044.stm

114 BBC News, 6th June 2007; http://news.bbc.co.uk/1/hi/world/europe/6727637.stm

115 *International Herald Tribune*, 29th December 2007; http://www.iht.com/articles/ap/2007/12/29/europe/EU-GEN-Italy-Libya-Immigration.php

116 *The Times*, 16th November 2007

In many ways this is the hardest of the three to answer. It is certainly a question that governments are reluctant to engage with, at least directly. Instead many countries, including now Britain, have adopted a qualitative rather than a quantitative approach. The idea is that rather than trying to work out how many immigrants to take each year, a country accepts those who meet predetermined educational requirements or have particular skills. The aim – though it is rarely spelled out – is to keep arrivals in check, while avoiding the need for a crude cap on numbers. The snag is that these schemes tend to be very bureaucratic, and unless they include some form of overall limit they may not do much to reduce numbers either. After years of denying that a cap on immigration is necessary the UK Government recently announced that it is thinking of introducing one.

But by far the most effective thing that Europe could do to curb immigration, legal or illegal, would be to improve the working of its own indigenous labour markets. As we will see in the next chapter, few older workers in Europe work right up to their official retirement age. Much more significant is that most European countries have high unemployment rates, especially among young people, yet still attract large numbers of migrants. This failure to make better use of their own workforces is the single most important pull factor that has boosted immigration into all the main European countries over the last 15 years.

At the top end of the labour market countries remain keen to poach talent and are happy to take doctors, engineers and other experts from wherever they can find them. Further down the scale industries like agriculture, construction and hospitality pay such low wages that often the only takers are illegal immigrants. According to the ONS, nine out of ten new jobs created over the last decade in this country went to foreign-born workers.[117] That this should have happened when so many of our own working-age people are not in employment is an extraordinary condemnation, both of the paucity of our skills base and of how the welfare system discourages benefit recipients from taking work. Why can't we train enough plumbers or provide enough waitresses of our own, instead of importing them? The inescapable conclusion is that recent immigra-

117 Labour Force Survey, Office for National Statistics, 2007

tion has had just as much to do with the weakness of our educational and welfare systems as it has the strength of the economy.

Many European countries have tried over the years to turn off the immigration tap. More often than not, the same countries have found themselves quietly having to switch the flow back on when growth picks up – Britain at the turn of the decade being a case in point. Unless the government is prepared to do more to improve the labour market in this country, the chances are that when growth resumes ministers will once again find themselves resorting to immigration as a quick fix for labour shortages. But turning off the immigration tap when growth slows, and then turning it back on when it recovers, has given us the worst of all worlds – an over-reliance on migrant labour *and* a shortage of skills and opportunities for our own indigenous workforce.

The bottom line is that immigrants will continue to come, legally or illegally, not just because they are desperate to escape the poverty of their own countries but also because they are coming to a place where they reckon they will find something to do. We cannot stop this, but what we can do is ensure that we need far fewer of them than we have recently been taking. It may not be easy politically, but the most effective way to curb immigration in the long term would be to reduce the demand for it, not by recession but by making far fuller use of the workers we already have.

Work Till You Drop

> No one is so old that he does not think he has a year to live.
> Cicero

If we are going to live longer it obviously makes sense, socially as well as financially, that we should work longer as well. Not everyone, however, will welcome being reminded of this. When politicians extol the virtues of flexible retirement, they usually speak in terms of self-fulfilment and financial advantage, but as a nation we work longer than our continental counterparts not because we want to, but because we have to. A survey in 2005 by the Employers Forum on Age, set up by the Government to encourage later retirement, found that most workers wanted to retire as soon as possible.[118] In Britain, though, this is becoming steadily harder. According to the OECD if you are over 65 and British you are almost five times as likely still to be working as you would be in France, and nearly twice as likely as in Germany.[119] For those retiring from the private sector and who have to rely on the state pension and the pension credit, the outlook is especially tough.

The pensioners stacking shelves in supermarkets rarely look very enthused, doing the sort of jobs they probably started out on 50 years before. But it is not just in Britain that people will increasingly have to work longer. In places where the pension age was previously 60 (or even below) the threshold is gradually being raised, usually to 65. In Britain, the pension age for women is set to rise from 60 to 65 between 2010 and 2020, and then to 68 for both sexes in 2048. In the US – despite its comparatively favourable demographics – the pension age for everybody is meant to rise to 67 by 2027. Reforms have also been introduced in many countries to make pensions less generous, or to persuade people to delay taking them up. Germany, France, Spain, Belgium, Sweden, Denmark and the UK are among those that will in future pay bonuses to those who defer retiring until after 65.[120]

In its report on ageing and public expenditure, the EU warned that:

> *Three distinct periods can be identified. Between 2004 and 2011, both demographic and employment developments will be supportive of growth: this period can be viewed as a window of opportunity for pursuing structural reforms. Between 2012 and 2017, rising employment rates will offset the decline in the working-age population: during this period, the working-age population will start to decline as the baby-boom generation enters retirement. The ageing effect will dominate as of 2018, and both the size of the working-age population and the number of persons employed will be on a downward trajectory.[121]*

118 *Attitude Not Age*, The Employers Forum on Age, 2005

119 Labour Force Survey, by sex and age, OECD

120 See table on p104

121 *The Impact of Aging on Public Expenditure*, The Economic Policy Committee and the European Commission, 2006a; http://europa.eu.int/comm/economy_finance/publications/eespecialreports_en.htm

With 2011 now just two years away, the window that the commission identified for reform is about to close.

But changing the established culture of retirement has proved difficult, as we have seen, and the results so far have been patchy and limited. Partly for this reason, pension reform timetables tend to be leisurely; in Britain the pension age will take four decades to get to 68. Other countries have similarly elongated schedules. The danger is that such plans will end up being too little too late, even if they can be delivered.

Nor are pensions the only problem. Unless we extend our working lives, most industrialised countries (not just those in Europe) could face severe labour shortages when the baby boomers retire as the chart on page 73 showed. In Japan, the population aged 15-64 is projected to fall by 20 million by 2035, or 25%, and Japan has little immigration to make up the difference. In America, the Bureau of Labor Statistics has predicted that between 2006 and 2016, the labour force will grow by some 8.5%: this is noticeably slower than the 12% growth of the previous decade and in 2007 (i.e. before the credit crunch) the Bureau was worried that it would not be enough to meet the demand for new workers caused by the imminent retirement of the baby boomers.[122]In Germany, Hungary, Bulgaria and several other Eastern European countries, working age populations are already falling. In many other EU states they are about to peak. It is this, just as much as the need to protect fragile welfare systems, that lies behind the drive to postpone retirement.

When the baby boomers' retire they will also take their skills with them, and many of them are very skilled indeed. A recent study by the German bank WestLB, citing a report from the country's Institute for the Study of Labour, estimated that by 2020 Germany will have to replace 45% of its engineers and nearly 35% of its lawyers, economists, mathematicians and scientists.[123]

Faced with predictions like these, the European Commission has, for some years, been urging its members to increase employment rates, not just by encouraging people to retire later but also by getting more people

122 *Employment Projections 2006-16,* US Bureau of Labor Statistics, 2007; http://www.bls.gov/news.release/History/ecopro.txt

123 *Corporate Ageing,* WestLB, June 2007

of working age into work. In fact, few Europeans actually work right up to their official pension age. Most retire, formally or informally, several years earlier.

Early retirement took off in the '80s and early '90s; as traditional industries were forced to shrink and restructure, letting older employees go early was seen as a humane way of reducing the headcount. State aid was often available to ease the transition and, after several decades of favourable demography, providing pensions for the early leavers was rarely a problem. So popular did early retirement prove that by the 1990s quitting in one's fifties had become the norm rather than the exception. In the 1970s the so-called participation rate of men aged 55-59 was 10% lower than that of other workers in most EU countries. By the turn of the century that gap had ballooned to 30%.[124]

When it comes to the real, as opposed to official, retirement age, the contrast between Europe and other developed countries is striking. In Italy men typically retire ten years earlier than in Japan, despite the two countries sharing the same adverse demography.

In Japan most people work well beyond the official pension age, the average real retirement age for men is 69 and 66 for women. In the US, the figures are 64 for men and 63 for women, very close to the official age. But in the EU, where most countries are now supposed to have a pension age of 65, the average man soldiers on to just 61 and the average woman to 60.[125]

It was not until the mid-90s that governments began to worry about the growing tendency of older workers to retire early and the unwillingness of employers to employ them. At first both were seen as more of a social problem than an economic issue, and older workers found themselves classified as another minority group in need of protection. The current emphasis on increasing the participation of older workers dates from the adoption in 2000 of the EU's Lisbon Agenda, which aimed to make Europe "the most dynamic and competitive knowledge-based economy in the world".

124 Report of the High Level Group on the future of social policy in an enlarged European Union, European Commission, May 2004

125 ibid

Country examples of pension reforms affecting timing of retirement

By increasing rewards and penalties associated with timing of retirement			
Country	Reform	Affecting whom	When
Australia	• Lump-sum bonus for deferral up to five years	All	1998
Austria	• Increase penalty for early retirement from 2% to 4.2% p.a.	All	1997
Belgium	• Higher pension fo deferring after 60 in public sector, up to 9% by age 65	All	2001
Denmark	• Pension reduction around 10% for retiring age 60-62	All	1999
	• Lump-sum bonus for working between 62 and 65	All	1999
	• Higher pensions for deferring after age 65 (e.g. +7% if defer to 66)	All	2004
Finland	• Flexible retirement age from 62 to 68 (7.2% bonus for delaying retirement to age 63 and 4.5% thereafter to age 68)	All	2005
France	• A bonus of 3% for each year the pension is postponed beyond age 60 (for those already at the full rate)	All	2004
	• Workers can draw a fraction of the pension while continuing to work under the scheme of progressive retirement	All	2005
Germany	• Pension 3.6% lower if retire aged 63-64; 6% higher for each year post-65	All	1997-2004
Italy	• Actuarially equivalent reductions from age 57	All	2015-2033
Spain	• Higher pension for retiring after 65; 2% for each year with no limit (for individuals with 35 years of contributions)	All	2002
Sweden	• Flexible retirement from age 61 with actuarially-based rewards/penalties for individuals with 35 years of Social Insurance contributions	All	1999
United Kingdom	• Higher pension for retiring between 65 and 70 raised from 7.5% to 10.4% for each year with lump-sum option added	All	2005

By restricting options for early retirement			
Country	**Reform**	**Affecting whom**	**When**
Austria	• From 60 to 61.5	Men	2000-2002
	• From 55 to 56.5	Women	2000-2002
	• From 56.5 to 61.5	Women	2018-2034
Belgium	• Require 35 rather 30 years contributions to retire early at 60.	All	1997-2005
Italy	• Seniority pensions for employees available from age 57 or with 40 years of contribution (previously from age 54-56 or with 37 years of contributions).	All	2002-2008

Source: *Live Longer, Work Longer,* OECD 2006

Since then progress has been slow. Figures from the EU employment report for 2006–07 show that the participation rate for older workers has risen from 39% to just 42% since 2001, against the Commission's target of 50% by 2010. The EU–wide average also hides huge disparities, in France under 40% of 55–64–year–olds were working in 2006. In Belgium, Italy, Hungary, Austria, Poland and several other East European countries the figure was less than a third. By contrast, in the US it was 64% and in Japan it was 67%.

It is much the same further down the age scale; getting Europeans to work more and longer can be done, but it is a slow process. As a continent we take longer holidays, work fewer hours or are more likely not to be working at all than people virtually anywhere else in the developed world:

• According to the ILO, Americans work between 1,800 and 2,000 hours a year, which is about the same as in Eastern Europe. But in Western Europe, we work far fewer. Among the big nations the UK puts in the longest hours at 1,600–1,800 a year, followed by France and Germany at fewer than 1,600.[126]

126 Key Indicators of the Labour Market, International; Labour Organisation, 2007; http://www.ilo.org/ public/english/employment/strat/kilm/download/kilm06.pdf

- Among 20-24 year olds, unemployment in the EU was 14% in 2007 but 8% or less in Australia, Japan and the US. In Italy it was 18%, France 17% and Spain 15%. Among the larger countries only Germany, at 11%, came anywhere near the non-European figure – and it has almost two million people on government-subsidised work schemes (see below).[127]

- Overall unemployment was also higher in Europe in 2007 than in other advanced countries, even before the credit crunch. It was 7.5% in the Euro Area, but less than 5% in Japan, the US and Australia. In Spain, France and Germany it was over 8%.[128]

- Some European countries, though by no means all, have low employment rates for women. In 2007, 69% of working-age women in the US were working, the same as in the UK, but the average in Europe was 59%. In Italy it was just 51%.[129]

Americans and Asians often point to figures like these to claim that Europeans are workshy. At first sight, they would seem to have a point. As well as retiring early we take a lot of paid holiday, typically four weeks or more in Europe, compared with two in the US. We also take more time off sick, nearly four weeks a year per worker in Sweden compared to less than a week in the US, according to a study by the think tank Open Europe.[130] And in some European countries, including Britain, very high numbers are off work permanently on health grounds.

But is it that we are lazy, or that over-regulation, rigid labour markets and poor skills prevent as many people working as would like to? Even before the economy weakened, if Europeans wanted a job it could be very difficult to find one because in most EU countries the labour markets are inflexible and inefficient. The large number of Europeans who have moved to Britain

---

127 Labour Force Survey, by sex and age, OECDhttp://stats.oecd.org/WBOS/Index.aspx?QueryName= 251&QueryType=View

128 Harmonised unemployment rate, OECDhttp://stats.oecd.org/WBOS/Index.aspx?QueryName=251& QueryType=View

129 Labour force survey by sex and age, OECDhttp://stats.oecd.org/WBOS/Index.aspx?QueryName=25 1&QueryType=View

130 *Beyond the European Social Model*, Open Europe, March 2006

in recent years to work in our comparatively liberal labour market were not lazy, and nor were they all from the poorer countries of Eastern Europe. Many came from affluent France, driven abroad by lack of opportunity in their own highly regulated and highly taxed economy.

In much of Europe, high marginal tax and social security rates on the one hand, and comparatively generous unemployment benefits on the other, mean that it is often simply not worth taking a job. The study by Open Europe found that "In Sweden, for someone going from being unemployed to earning 1,500 euros a month the difference between what they would have received out of work to what they would have received in work is only 5 euros a day."[131]

The situation is much the same in Germany, and only a little better in France where employers are discouraged from taking more people on by the high level of protection and entitlements they have to provide. Europeans often denounce what they see as the brutal hire-and-fire mentality of Anglo-American capitalism. But if employers cannot lay people off, they will be much less likely to hire them in the first place. The result is not only that unemployment is high in many European countries, but many people remain unemployed for an unhealthily long time.

In Britain, an extraordinarily high 2.8 million people are off work on Incapacity Benefit. Before the recent decline in the economy, this number was double the official unemployment figure and had been so for some years.[132] In Germany over half the unemployed in 2007 had been jobless for more than a year.[133] Hidden unemployment is another problem. In France around a million people were on government subsidised employment schemes of one sort or another in 2008, and in Germany the number was nearly two million.[134]

For years, economists and commentators have been urging Europe to do more about the problems in its labour markets. Faced with the imminent decline of its workforce and the retirement of the baby boomers, politicians know that action is essential. But they also know that their

131 ibid
132 Labour Market Statistics, Office for National Statistics, 2008
133 Eurostat Yearbook, 2008
134 ibid

voters remain deeply suspicious of reform for the simple reason that the majority are in work and believe that the status quo protects them.

Pensions, retirement ages, job security, entitlement to sick pay – these and others like them are very delicate issues, bedevilled by vested interests and entrenched attitudes which politicians challenge at their peril. For governments, including Britain's, it has often been easier to fall back on the quick fix of immigration than to tackle the deep-seated problems in their labour markets. Over the next few years, the pressures of recession will probably make reform even harder. In the medium term, however, if we are to overcome the huge economic hurdle posed by the retirement of the baby boomers, without resort to further mass immigration, then Europe's governments will have to get to grips with their labour markets. With the age crunch almost upon us, they have already left it desperately late.

The Baby Famine

> There is no finer investment for any community than putting milk into babies.
> Winston Churchill

Over the last 15 years fertility in many European countries has fallen to unprecedented levels. Italy and Spain were the first to drop to the lowest-low level of fertility, a TFR of 1.3, and remain there or thereabouts for a sustained period. Today, 16 out of the 27 nations of the EU have a TFR of 1.5 or less, and between them they account for over half its total population. The only other region in the world to experience a baby famine on this scale is East Asia where birth rates in Japan, South Korea, Hong Kong and Singapore have plunged to similar depths.

In countries where the birth rate has now been below replacement level for two generations, the risk is that the process will feed on itself. Demographers at the University of Pennsylvania have calculated that at a sustained TFR of 1.3 the number of births would halve in just 45 years.[135] Forty-five years, these days, represents probably a generation and a half.

135 Kohler H-P, Billari F and Ortega J, *Low and Lowest-Low Fertility in Europe: Causes, Implications and Policy Options,* University of Pennsylvania, 2005

Over two full generations, say 60 years, the maths is even more dramatic. If a cohort of two million people (men and women) reproduces at the rate of 1.3 children per woman they will have between them approximately 650,000 girls. If these girls in turn reproduce at the same rate as their parents, they will have 845,000 children in total and so on until, surprisingly quickly, you have very few people left at all.

This is the prospect the Italians now face. Happily, in Northern and Western Europe we are more fecund and our prospects of avoiding extinction are better. If you do the same sum but using a TFR of 1.75 children per woman, you end up after two generations with a drop from two million to just over one and a half million. This is still a significant decline, but one that should be manageable with limited immigration and better use of the indigenous labour force.

We have of course been here before, in the '30s and '40s when low fertility produced very much the same sort of gloomy projections that we see now. Today, however, the UN is projecting that birth rates in the lowest fertility countries will recover significantly over the next half-century. Could it turn out to be right, or is it being over optimistic? In the UN's favour it should be said that it is not alone in thinking that low fertility could cure itself. In the US writers like Phillip Longman have observed that the more religious and right wing a person is, the more children they are likely to have. From this they deduce that we may be returning to a more "patriarchal" world".[136] The theory goes that because most people end up following much the same lifestyle and holding much the same beliefs as their parents, an ever increasing proportion of the population will come from these larger families.

It is a theory that has found favour with some on the American right who hope that eventually, if such families again become the norm, God-fearing Republicans should outbreed secular, liberal Democrats. And it is the case that birth rates in religious, Republican-voting states in the mid-West and South are significantly higher than for their counterparts in more secular, Democrat states on the East and West coasts.[137] However,

136 Longman P, op cit

137 *Wall Street Journal*, 22nd August 2007

the trend is comparatively new, and a much more important reason for America's buoyant birth rate is the high fertility of Hispanics – who do not fit easily into secular v religious, Right v Left categorisations.

Nor is there much sign of anything similar happening in Europe or, indeed, anywhere else in the world. Most regions where religious fervour is strong or growing (like South America and the Muslim world) have falling birth rates. In increasingly secular Europe it is the most religious countries that generally have the lowest fertility. Even if the patriarchal theory might work for the US, it would seem to be the exception rather than the rule.

Another, more prosaic and Eurocentric approach points out that lowest-low fertility often goes together with limited employment and housing opportunities for young people. As the number of young people declines, eventually they should face less competition for jobs and homes. This, in turn, should mean that they are able to set up on their own, and start breeding, more quickly. In the European context this sounds more plausible, but it is as yet entirely untested. There is also the problem that even if finding jobs and homes does become easier for young Europeans, by the time they have paid (via taxation) for their parents' pensions and healthcare, there may not be much left over for having children.

Yet another suggestion is that immigration could boost fertility, as it has in both Britain and the US. But in Spain and Italy – both high immigration countries – the TFR has hardly budged over the last decade. Meanwhile France worries that its comparatively high fertility is disproportionately due to its large North African community, even though current levels of immigration into the country are quite low. The experience of most Western countries has anyway been that the fertility of immigrants groups fairly soon falls into line with that of their host country. Even where immigration does boost birth rates, the effect is likely to be short lived.

If countries afflicted by very low fertility are to find a remedy, it looks as if they are going to have to find it for themselves, rather than just waiting for birth rates – or young immigrants – to turn up. This is where all those factors and influences that lead women to delay having children – dubbed "competitors" by demographers – come into the equation. As was discussed briefly in the Introduction, everybody knows, at least in general terms, why women in the developed world are having so few babies compared with previous generations. Modern contraception, better educational, career and economic opportunities for women, increased sexual equality, the expense of bringing up children, all these have played their part in the recent decline in fertility rates. Today there are plenty of worthwhile and profitable things for a woman to do as well as bring up children. "Competitors" is an apposite term, and the impact they have had on fertility is clear right across the developed world.

First, and most important, the age at which women start to have children has risen significantly over the last 35 years. The postponement of motherhood has happened in all industrialised countries but it has been most marked in Europe, first in the West and now in the East as well. As the table below shows, what is known as the "mean age at first birth" is now higher in all the main Western European countries (except France) than it is even in Japan – and significantly higher than in the US.

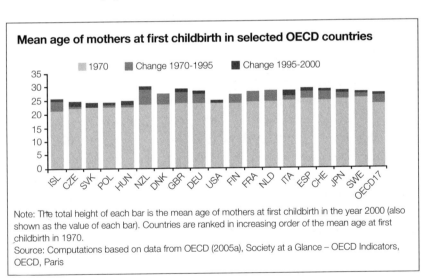

Mean age of mothers at first childbirth in selected OECD countries

Note: The total height of each bar is the mean age of mothers at first childbirth in the year 2000 (also shown as the value of each bar). Countries are ranked in increasing order of the mean age at first childbirth in 1970.
Source: Computations based on data from OECD (2005a), Society at a Glance – OECD Indicators, OECD, Paris

But while the fertility of women in their twenties has fallen, that of women in their thirties has risen, often sharply. In England and Wales in

1977 women aged 25–29 were twice as likely to have babies as those aged
30–34. Today, it is those between 30–34 who have the most babies, while
the 35–39 group have almost as many as the 20–24s.[138]

Crucially, however, fertility among older women has not risen enough to
make up for the lower number of children women have when they are young.
As a result, not only is the overall birth rate lower than it was, but families are
smaller than they used to be – as shown in the next table from the OECD.

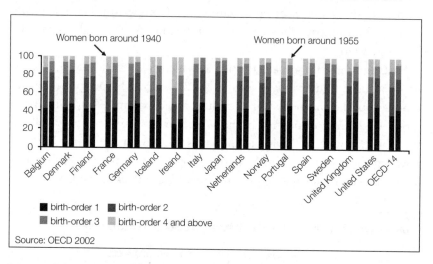

Source: OECD 2002

None of this is unexpected. But another result of women postponing birth
perhaps is: they are having fewer children than they wanted – or at least
say they wanted. Surprising though it may be, given how birth rates have
fallen, surveys on the subject show that European women would like to
have, on average, two children apiece. The same goes for other low fertility
countries like Japan and South Korea. The OECD chart below gives the
difference between desired and actual fertility across a range of countries.

If such surveys are right then the nub of the fertility dilemma facing the
continent is that women are not only having fewer children than they used to,
but also that they are having fewer than they say they would like to. To put
it another way, if European women were to have the average of two children
they say they would like, there would be no European population problem.

138 Fertility statistics, Office for National Statistics, 2008; http://www.statistics.gov.uk/cci/nugget.
asp?ID=951

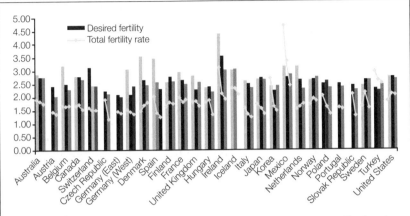

Observed fertility rate is measured by the total fertility rate of each country in that year. The three bars shown for each country refer to data for 1981, 1990 and 2000, with the exceptions of Austria, the Czech Republic and the eastern Länder of Germany, (where data refer to 1990 and 2000), and of Switzerland, Poland and Turkey (where the data refer to 1990, 1995 and 2000).
Source: Data from the World Values Survey (1981, 1990, 2000) and Eurobarometer (2002) as in European Foundation (2004).

So how can women be persuaded or tempted to have more children, especially in the very low fertility countries? A generation ago, demographers came up with a theory called the Second Demographic Transition, to explain why fertility continued to fall after countries had made the transition from an agricultural to an industrial economy. The classic theory of demographic transition had assumed that, once industrialisation was complete, fertility would settle at around the replacement rate and population would stabilise. It failed to foresee the sustained low fertility that now characterises most of the developed world.

According to the Population Reference Bureau (PRB), the Second Demographic Transition occurs when "fertility falls below the two-child replacement level as forces of contemporary life interfere with childbearing. This transition has been linked with greater educational and job opportunities for women, the availability of effective contraception, a shift away from formal marriage, the acceptance of childbearing outside marriage, and the rise of individualism and materialism."[139] Anyone surveying contemporary Europe would recognise this picture. But even so, it does not quite ring true.

139 *Transitions in World Population,* Population Reference Bureau, 2004

Why is it, for instance, that some countries in Europe have so much higher fertility than others when their lifestyles, attitudes and economies seem, at least on the surface, to be so similar? And why is it that, contrary to what the PRB suggests, the countries in which fertility has fallen farthest have been the most socially conservative, like Italy, Spain or Poland, rather than the more socially progressive countries of North and Western Europe?

It is only on closer examination that it becomes apparent how widely circumstances and attitudes to marriage, illegitimacy and working mothers still vary from country to country within Europe, and how these factors relate to fertility levels. What appears to distinguish most of the very low fertility countries are:

- Poor job opportunities for young people and especially for young women. In 1999 the three EU countries with the worst youth unemployment also had the lowest fertility. [140] The unemployment rate in 2006 for women aged 15-24 in Italy was 27%, in Greece it was 29%. For men it was 38 and 36% respectively.

- A rapid recent rise in the number of young people enrolling in further education. This soared in all of Europe's very-low-fertility countries in the 1990s – perhaps because jobs were so scarce. Again, this was especially marked for women. Between 1989 and 1999 the percentage of women enrolling in university rose from 25 to 56 % in Greece, from 33 to 63% in Spain, from 14 to 29% in the Czech Republic, from 15 to 40% in Hungary, and from 8 to 24% in Romania.[141]

- A high proportion of young people living at home. A study in 2001 found that in Denmark, half of all young men have left home before they are 22, while in Italy it is not until almost age 30 that half of all men have left home. The equivalent ages for women were 20 in Denmark and 27 in Italy.[142]

140 Del Boca D, *Why are Fertility Rates so Low in Italy and Southern Europe?* University of Turin, presented at the Italian Academy, University of Columbia, 2003

141 ibid

142 Iacovou M, op cit (November 2001) *Leaving home in the European Union*, Working Papers for the institute of social and economic research, paper 2001-18. Colchester: University of Essex

- A traditional attitude to marriage and illegitimacy. Very-low-fertility countries tend to be socially conservative, and their level of births out of wedlock has risen far more slowly than in other advanced countries, as the graph below shows.

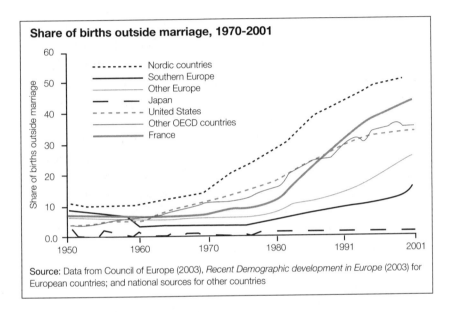

Share of births outside marriage, 1970-2001

Legend:
- Nordic countries
- Southern Europe
- Other Europe
- Japan
- United States
- Other OECD countries
- France

Source: Data from Council of Europe (2003), *Recent Demographic development in Europe* (2003) for European countries; and national sources for other countries

If a woman, before she feels ready to have a child, has first to go to university, subsequently find a job and a place to live, and finally get married, it is perhaps not surprising that in all the very low fertility countries the mean age at first birth (MAFB) has risen sharply. Between 1980 and 2000 the MAFB in Greece rose from 24 to 27, in Italy from 25 to nearly 29 and in Spain from 25 to over 29. In Eastern Europe, the MAFB barely budged in the 1980s under communism, but then rose significantly in the '90s.[143]

Nevertheless, postponement cannot be the whole explanation for these countries' low birth rates. While the trend has been more recent and rapid in Southern and Eastern Europe, it is something that all developed countries now have in common, even the US. In this respect, Southern

143 D'Addio A and D'Ercole M, *Trends and Determinants of Fertility Rates in OECD countries: the Role of Policies,* OECD, 2005

and Eastern Europe have really been doing no more than catching up with what had already happened in the more advanced North and West. Britain's MAFB at 29.1 in 2000 was exactly the same as Spain's, and that of the Netherlands was the same as Italy's.

To understand why fertility has fallen so much further in Southern and Eastern Europe than it has in the North and West, and also why it has stayed so low when in the North and West birth rates are showing signs of recovery, we have to look at what happens after – rather than before – a woman's first baby. In particular, we need to look at how easy it is for a new mother to combine having a child with the lifestyle and employment opportunities that were previously available to her.

This, too, varies greatly from country to country. Part of it is social and cultural, part economic, but the key seems to be the ease or otherwise of combining motherhood and employment. Even in socially conservative countries, if a woman has to give up her job in order to become a mother she stands to lose money, status, independence and the stimulation of going out to work. And even if she is prepared to do this for one baby, she may not be prepared to do it for two or more.

Across Europe, a woman's chances of being able to combine motherhood with a job depend crucially on:

• Whether society encourages working mothers or frowns on them.

• A flexible labour market, which she can leave and re-enter relatively easily, and which offers part-time as well as full-time jobs. Such jobs are easier to find if unemployment is low and the service sector well developed.

• Good childcare; the cheaper, more flexible and readily available the better.

• A reasonably high level of financial support from the state in the form of maternity leave, child support, day care etc. As the OECD chart below shows, low fertility Italy, Spain and Greece are among the lowest spenders on family benefits. Conversely France, Sweden and the UK all spend more than average on them.

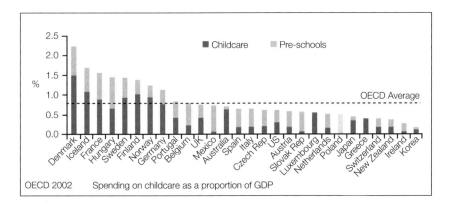

OECD 2002   Spending on childcare as a proportion of GDP

Not all of this, it should be stressed, is in the gift of government. Legislation, rights and public spending play a part in encouraging fertility, but so do social attitudes and the health of the economy. The following table, taken from a 2003 paper on Italy's low fertility by Daniela del Boca of the University of Turin, throws a fascinating light on how the burden on working mothers is eased in higher fertility countries by both the availability of part-time work and the willingness of fathers to help with housework – and how much tougher life is for working mothers in Southern Europe.[144]

	Weekly Hours	% Male Housework
Sweden	30	33
Netherlands	25.5	35
UK	30.7	33
Germany	27.5	36
France	34	33
Italy	34.6	19
Spain	36	12
Greece	37.8	12

In many very low fertility countries, it seems to be the combination of inflexible labour markets, conservative social attitudes *and* modern consumer culture that represents the biggest obstacle to raising fertility. But

144 Del Boca D, op cit

it would be wrong to assume that even in the very low fertility countries nothing can be done to boost birth rates. Not only are some policies and attitudes clearly detrimental to fertility, there is also strong evidence from several European countries that non-coercive pro-natalist measures can achieve at least modest increases in the birth rate in democratic societies.

Governments, it has to be said, have rarely succeeded when they have tried to encourage their citizens to have more children – either voluntarily or by coercion. Demographers call it pro-natalism, and it was first given a bad name by Mussolini and Hitler. Post-1945, the most notorious attempt by a European government to boost its population occurred in Romania, under the Ceausescu regime. In 1966 virtually all forms of birth control and abortion were banned by decree overnight, and the Romanian birth rate doubled in the space of a year. In the 1980s, as it fell back to its previous level, these draconian measures were further strengthened, with all employed women under 40 required to undergo monthly gynaecological examinations while unmarried persons over 25 and voluntarily childless couples were subjected to a new, punitive level of taxation. Finally, in 1984 the minimum marriage age for women was lowered to 15, but all to no avail. After its initial surge in the late 1960s, Romania's birth rate returned stubbornly to much the same level as that of its neighbours and stayed there.[145]

But just because pro-natalism was associated with fascism and communism, this should not mean that we should give up all hope of boosting Europe's low birth rates. Over two or three decades, small incremental changes in fertility could have a big impact.

In Germany, the main problem, as we have seen, is the number of women who remain childless – a third of those aged 40. According to Germany's (female) family minister Ursula von der Leyen: "The question is not whether women will work. They will work. The question is whether they will have kids."[146] To encourage parenthood, the Government spends quite a lot on family benefits. German mothers

145 Country Studies, Romania, Demographic Policy, Federal Research Division of the Library of Congress; http://www.countrystudies.com/romania/demographic-policy.html

146 *International Herald Tribune*, 24th April 2006; http://www.iht.com/articles/2006/04/23/news/germany.php

are entitled to 14 weeks' paid maternity leave starting six weeks before childbirth, but whilst seemingly generous, this does not compare well to the rest of the OECD; in France it is 16 weeks and in the UK it is 26 weeks.[147] However, Germany does spend a significant amount on childcare, at over $3,000 a child. Yet fertility remains obstinately stuck just above the 1.3 level. One, major reason is that the labour market is not very family friendly. In Sweden nearly 90% of mothers (with at least one child under 16) are employed, in Germany it is under 60%.[148] Many German schools also finish at lunchtime, which makes life difficult for mothers who want to work.

In Italy, many young people choose to study for extended periods rather than look for a job they know they will not find, and continue to live with their parents well into their thirties. Even if a young person can find a job, housing is expensive and mortgages are difficult to get – none of which encourages parenthood. The Italian Government talks about trying to boost the birth rate, but according to the OECD its position on fertility is still one of "no intervention".[149] At the moment in Europe, of the large West European countries only Spain spends less on family benefits than Italy.[150] Deregulating the banking system, to make mortgages more easily available, would probably do more to increase the country's fertility, but right up to the credit crunch the Italian government was doing all it could to thwart EU pressure to open its banks up to foreign takeover and competition. Like many other countries, Italy has not just been slow to respond to its population crisis, but also reluctant.

Spain's prognosis is, if anything, even worse than Italy's, despite its high immigration. Up to 1975 family policy was very conservative under the Franco regime, even by the standards of Southern Europe. Contraception was banned and women were honoured for staying at home and raising

---

147 Family Database, OECD; http://www.oecd.org/dataoecd/45/26/37864482.pdf
148 ibid
149 ibid
150 Family Database, OECD, op cit

large families. And this policy appeared to get results; Spanish fertility pre-1975 was consistently around three children a woman, compared to an EU average at the time of just over two.

From the late 1970s all this changed as democracy was established. The official attitude to the family became very much "hands off" and fertility began to fall steeply, dropping below the replacement rate around 1980, below the EU average five years later, and finally bottoming out at below 1.2 in 1998. Since then the TFR has recovered, but only marginally.

Spanish fertility has fallen for much the same reasons as in Italy – high youth unemployment, high house prices meaning that young people are living with their parents for longer and marrying later, and strong disapproval of cohabitation and illegitimacy. Reaction against Franco's policy has also played a part and, until very recently, discouraged a more proactive approach to family policy.[151] Spain spends a little over 1% of GDP on family benefits, whether it is cash payments, tax breaks or childcare services - one of the lowest figures in the EU. Spanish politicians are belatedly waking up to the gravity of the country's demographic crisis. As in Italy, however, there is little sign as yet that they are ready to do very much about it.

The country that is usually reckoned to have done best recently at raising fertility is France, whose TFR has increased from 1.65 in 1993 to over 1.9 today, placing it second only to Ireland in the EU. The French have a much longer and stronger tradition of family policy than most other European countries, summed up by the comment of the development minister Gilles de Robien in 2005 that "demography is a very great source of vitality for France".[152] Paid maternity leave was first introduced in 1913, and in 1939 the Family Code was adopted in response to deep seated worries over a birth rate that had lagged its neighbours for a century.

Official policy has been overtly pro-natalist ever since. Today, it is best known for the generous financial incentives available for third and subse-

---

151 University of Columbia, Clearinghouse on International Developments in Child, Youth and Family Policies, 2004Clearinghouse on International Developments in Child, Youth and Family Policies

152 *Population Politics,* Institute of Public Policy Research, 9th February 2006

quent children. The allowance for having a third child has recently more than doubled up to 1,000 euros per month for the first year.[153] Larger families are entitled to longer parental leave, special housing allowances and enhanced cash benefits. In Europe, France is second only to Denmark when it comes to spending on childcare.[154] Workers in the large public sector can get even more help; not long ago a police inspector, who published a book on the Beatles, revealed that he had spent 12 of the last 18 years on paid paternity leave, thanks to his *famille nombreuse*.[155]

Despite its relatively high unemployment and notoriously inflexible labour market, another area where France scores highly is in enabling women to combine work and motherhood. Public childcare is affordable and widely available; the *école maternelle,* entitles every child in France to state funded pre-school education, and the take up is over 90%.[156] In addition nearly 82% of all women aged 25-49 are employed.[157]

Sweden is another European country often cited for its (relatively) high fertility. Swedish policy has never been as overtly pro-natalist as France, instead the emphasis has always been on promoting gender equality and equal access to work. Britain also does well in this regard, with a good supply of both part-time jobs and accessible childcare. The introduction by Labour tax credits, together with more generous rates of income support for workless households with children, has also been credited with helping to boost the TFR over the last few years.[158] A more detailed discussion of whether Britain is family friendly or not can be found in the conclusion.

Looking beyond Europe, it is interesting to contrast how ultra-low-fertility Japan and the demographically buoyant United States view the

---

153 BBC News, "France Claims EU Fertility Crown", 16th January 2007; http://news.bbc.co.uk/1/hi/world/europe/6268251.stm

154 Family Database, Public Spending on Childcare and Early Education, OECD 2003, see www.oecd.org/els/social/family/database

155 *The Daily Telegraph*, 8th October 2005

156 *Starting Strong, Early Childhood Education and Care,* OECD, 2006

157 National Institute for Statistics and Economic Studies (INSEE), November 2007; http://www.insee.fr/en/ffc/chifcle_fiche.asp?tab_id=303

158 *Welfare Reform: the impact on fertility*, Research in Public Policy, 2008

fertility question. In Japan, virtually every ministry has a taskforce considering how to boost the birth rate. Central government, municipalities and even many companies offer bonuses and other inducements to have second or third babies, but to little avail. Employer groups have even suggested the government campaign to encourage illegitimacy.[159] More conventional schemes such as that of the carmaker, Daihatsu, which offered employees who had a fourth child £1,000 and free car rental for three years, have proved no more successful. In fact, that particular offer did not get a single taker. [160]

Perhaps that should not come as a surprise when the country's highly educated young women often earn more than men, making neither marriage nor children a very attractive prospect; in one poll 70% of Japanese single women said they did not want to get married.[161] Yet traditional views on the family remain extremely strong; just 1% of Japanese births occur outside wedlock – even lower than the figure in Southern and Eastern Europe. Meanwhile the Japanese government professes huge concern at the situation, but spends 70% of its welfare budget on programmes for the elderly, compared to 4% on services for parents, including childcare. According to the OECD, Japanese public spending on family benefits is lower even than that of Spain and Italy.

In America public spending on family measures is also low, at least compared with Europe. Combined federal and state expenditure on all forms of family benefit is only marginally higher than Japan's, while the cash benefits for parents are the lowest of any OECD nation. There is no national paid maternity leave, although some states do have publicly funded programmes.[162] Nor is there any obligation on employers to fill the gap, although all companies with more than 50 employees have to allow unpaid maternity leave. In general support for parenthood is concentrated on tax breaks for low paid parents and there is also some

159 *The Guardian*, 3rd February 2002; http://www.guardian.co.uk/world/2002/feb/03/jonathanwatts. theobserver

160 *The Guardian*, 2nd August 2001; http://www.guardian.co.uk/world/2001/aug/02/population.jonathanwatts

161 BBC News, 25th February 2005;http://news.bbc.co.uk/1/hi/world/asia-pacific/4296877.stm

162 *Maternity Leave in the United States,* Institute for Women's Policy Research, August 2007

public funding for childcare, though nothing like as much as in most European countries.[163]

Yet America remains the most fertile of all industrialised countries. Part of this, as we have already seen, can be put down to the high fecundity of the rapidly growing Hispanic community. Even more important, though, is the openness and flexibility of the US economy and labour market: part-time jobs are plentiful and flexible (or were, before the credit crunch), taking up work and leaving it is easy and unbureaucratic, shops and other services remain open for long hours. There is probably no other advanced country in which it is as simple for a woman to combine work with having children, even though most of the part-time jobs that American working mothers rely on are not at all well paid. The contrast with Japan and parts of Europe, as regards both attitudes and opportunities, could hardly be starker.

The American experience, although very different from the European in many respects, confirms what numerous studies have found on this side of the Atlantic: to feel confident about embarking on parenthood young people need to have a place of their own, financial independence and, for mothers, the chance to work flexibly. They should also have a good chance of achieving this by their mid-twenties, and not be under too much pressure to get married before having a baby.

These are by far the most important pre-conditions for raising fertility in any advanced economy. But for socially conservative societies with heavily regulated labour markets they can pose a huge a challenge. Even in countries afflicted by very low fertility, people see little reason to make the changes that will be necessary to encourage more children. This is not just a matter of vested economic interests resisting reform – although that is certainly part of it. In many countries any concerted effort to raise fertility would soon run up against all sorts of deeply held political and moral views. The Left is never going to take kindly to the idea of deregulating working practices. Nor will it easily accept that public spending and taxes may have to be curbed in the interest of intergenerational fairness, if young people are to be encouraged to have more children. The Right and the Catholic church find it equally hard to accept that, across Europe,

163 For detailed discussion see Bradshaw J. and Finch N, *A Comparison of Child Benefit Packages in 22 Countries*, Department for Work and Pensions Research Report No 174, 2002

single parenthood and a high proportion of working mothers seem to go hand-in-hand with a higher birth rate.

Like it or not, however, these are the issues that go to the heart of the fertility dilemma. Any European country that ignores them does so at its peril.

Conclusion

Perfect numbers like perfect men are very rare.
Rene Descartes

The credit crunch was not caused by the demographic crunch; indeed, at least at this stage, it is hard to discern many links between them. But, whatever the outcome of the current turmoil, Britain and Europe are likely to emerge from the credit crunch only to find that they are at the beginning of a long demographic crunch. In Europe, people have never had it so good and they have never, in modern times, had so few babies. As we have become more comfortable, the basic human urge to reproduce, which has survived famine, pestilence and war, is faltering in the face of peace and prosperity. This is the paradox behind the continent's looming demographic deficit.

Over the next 40 years we will struggle to cope with ageing, stagnating and falling populations, just as much of the rest of the world is surging ahead. This shifting of the demographic plates will lead to huge changes, which, even now, people are only just beginning to think about. With a bit of luck, technology and trade will once again boost living standards even in those countries worst affected by population change, as they have with such spectacular effect over the last two decades. However, even with luck on its side, Europe is going to be facing ever stronger countervailing forces. Given the demographic pressures on the continent, reform of its ossified economy is more likely to be a matter of survival, not a chance to regain its lost pre-eminence.

History suggests that demography can go in cycles. But the decline in fertility affecting much of Europe today does not feel cyclical. In many countries birth rates appear to be stuck at dangerously low levels and their populations are ageing at an alarming rate. If these countries' demography is going to improve, it will need a nudge. Politicians in western countries are deeply nervous of telling women to have more children – and rightly so. Even a dictatorship cannot force parenthood on its people, as Ceausescu discovered in Romania. But while pressure will not work, encouragement could. Countries whose populations are ageing or declining need to make parenthood a priority, rather than an afterthought as it generally is now.

What form that might take will depend on the particular circumstances of each country – social, cultural, economic and political. There can be no single pan-European solution for the problems of European demography. But for much of the continent the options really are pretty stark, and time is running short. Europe badly needs to get younger. Either Germany, Italy, Poland, Spain *et al* rediscover the urge to reproduce, or they will soon have to reconcile themselves to becoming weaker and less numerous, and very possibly poorer as well.

Britain

A Stable Population

Unlike these countries, Britain does not face the prospect that its indigenous population could halve over the next few generations. Indeed, compared with most of Europe the demographic dilemma facing us is relatively unthreatening. But, as this book has sought to explain, the challenges posed by our demography are real enough, and nor can we expect to remain immune to the difficulties that are going to bedevil many of our neighbours.

Hence the question of whether Britain needs a population policy. Many countries have such a policy, but the official attitude in this country has, for a long time, been one of benign neglect. The consequences of this are now coming home to roost. Throwing our doors open to mass immigration while allowing so many of our own working age population to languish on benefit has not proved a good idea. Increasing taxes on the young to fund ever-rising spending on the old, another feature of current government policy, looks equally unsustainable.

An all-embracing population policy would probably be too complicated to be practicable, but that does not mean we should have no opinion on what size of population we want, or how we might influence it. The

options were listed in the introduction: in economic terms, growing populations have generally been advantageous; on environmental grounds,
there is an obvious case for trying to shrink our numbers; as far as social
cohesion and fairness between the generations are concerned, there is a
lot to be said for a stable population.

Unless fertility suddenly takes off, the first option, of a growing population, would have to rely on immigration. But even Labour, which has, in
effect, pursued an open door policy for much of the last decade, now says
it wants to reduce the number of people settling here. What of the second
option, a shrinking population? In theory, this might be attractive if it really
meant less congestion and pollution, but on closer examination the draw-
backs become apparent. We can hardly emulate China's one-child policy.
Nor has anyone yet worked out an effective answer to Keynes's point,
about how to reduce population without massive economic dislocation.

Even the third option, of staying roughly as we are, will not be as
straightforward as it might sound. As the baby boomers move into retirement, the British population is set to age uncomfortably fast even
if it is still expanding. Whatever happens to immigration, or any other
aspect of our population, in demographic terms we are in for a bumpy
couple of decades.

Looking further forward, however, it would take only a comparatively
small increase in our current fertility level to provide a population that
would be broadly stable. In books on demography populations are often
shown as pyramids, with a large number of younger people at the base
supporting a smaller number of old at the top. Over the last 30 years the
populations of most European countries have increasingly started to re-
semble inverse pyramids, as the old have begun to outnumber the young.
The population we should aim for is one in which each generation is
of roughly the same size as that below and above it — a column, rather
than a pyramid. If we could achieve this, the advantages, not just for the
sustainability of welfare, health and other social systems, but also for the
economy in general, for the environment and for fairness between the
generations, would be considerable.

Scotland now has an explicit population target and the UK Government
should consider drawing up one too. At the very least we need a strategy

to deal with the demographic challenges we are going to be facing over the next few decades. This should not be so much a matter of trying to devise an all embracing policy to guide the future course of our population, more a matter of making sure that it's at the forefront of government thinking.

As a first step, the Government should set up a new Royal Commission on Population, not so much to shape such a strategy but to inform it. The 270-page report of the postwar commission provides a model for a comprehensive review of population policy. It linked up everything from welfare to town planning to the implications of demographics for foreign policy. It is time for another such exercise today. Politicians often talk of the need for joined up government; demography is an area that needs it more than most.

Fertility

A stable population, however, will only be possible if we can boost our birth rate that extra bit. Simply urging British women to have more children will not do the trick. Judging by the experience of those countries that have tried it, straight bribery would be unlikely to work either. To be effective, the sort of mild pro-natalism that could help to achieve this will have to be subtle.

Fertility, as we have seen, is affected by a huge range of issues and new factors come into play all the time; the availability of jobs, childcare and housing, attitudes to women working, to marriage and traditional morality are just some of them. Where Britain scores well is on the availability of part-time work, and the general flexibility of our labour market. Gordon Brown's tax credit system, with its emphasis on helping single mothers into work, can be regarded as modestly pro-natal even though it has been criticised on other grounds.[164] Britain is also very relaxed about births outside marriage. Again, many commentators deplore the social consequences of this and, in particular, the role played in it by the benefits system. Nevertheless the experience of countries with a less relaxed attitude towards the traditional family suggests that Britain's easy-going approach is one of the main reasons our birth rate remains comparatively robust.

164 Hakim C, Bradley K, Price E and Mitchell L, *Little Britons: Financing Childcare Choice,* Policy Exchange, 2008

Where we score badly is on inter-generational fairness. Student debt, stamp duty, petrol duty and council tax all fall disproportionately on young families. All have risen sharply over the last decade, with much of the money spent on pensions and healthcare for the elderly. The cost of housing is another disincentive to having children, even allowing for the current downturn. In many areas prices have soared because supply has not been allowed to keep up with demand. This may help elderly downsizers, but it makes it far more difficult for young people to set up on their own, a crucial precursor to having children. Other aspects of environmental policy can also be unwittingly anti-family. As well as housing, parents need cheap food and cheapish petrol, but the powerful green lobby is deeply suspicious of all three. The school system is another problem area. Concern over the quality of schools and access to the better ones may not deter couples from having their first child, but they are yet another discouragement for those who might be contemplating a larger family.

It is not that British politicians want to discourage people from having children – far from it. But because fertility is not high up their agenda, other things take precedence. The danger is that if we do not actively encourage parenthood, the birth rate will not just stand still but slip down to continental levels. The government should never tell people how many children to have. But, provided they are non-coercive, policies that aim to encourage a higher fertility are perfectly legitimate, and the evidence from countries like France is that they can also be effective.

Currently the British TFR, at 1.9 children per woman, is the highest it has been for 30 years. But whereas the TFR for foreign-born women is 2.1, for indigenous women it is 1.75. If immigration falls, therefore, it seems likely that the TFR could fall back too. Nevertheless, even if one takes the indigenous TFR of 1.75, it would only take a 20% uplift to get it up to replacement level. This should not be an unreasonable or unduly ambitious target to aim for.

Immigration and Labour Market Reform

As we have seen, the availability of jobs plays an important role in determining a country's fertility. And in Britain, especially at a time of recession, there are growing fears that the less skilled will not be able to find them if we continue to accept so many immigrants. This has led to a lively debate over cause and effect: are the incomers taking jobs that would otherwise go to British workers, or is the real problem that the British are too lazy or unskilled to do the work themselves?

Interesting though it may be, this argument is largely irrelevant. Relying on immigration as an economic quick fix has given us the worst of both worlds. It has led us to neglect our own workforce, while at the same time becoming over dependent on migrant labour. That the overwhelming majority of new jobs should have been taken by immigrants over the last decade, while millions of working-age Britons have languished on benefits, is a scandal whichever way you look at it.

Better border controls, points systems etc. are all very well, but there is little we can really do about the push factors that drive migrants to leave their own countries – particularly in the third world. Immigrants, though, go where they think they are needed, and here we can have some influence. We have to reform our welfare system to ensure that far fewer British people of working age are left to live their lives on benefits. And we have to improve our education system to ensure that all our young people enter adulthood motivated to work and furnished with the basic skills employers require.

In the meantime, immigrants will continue to come and continue to be needed. Given this, it probably would be sensible to impose a cap on the number of arrivals. Admittedly any such number would be fairly arbitrary, but at least we would then have a benchmark to measure the level of immigration by, and try to adjust it accordingly. A points-based entry system, of the sort that has just been introduced in this country, is unlikely to be effective without some sort of overall limit.

Above all, however, we have to understand that the key to controlling immigration is to reduce the demand for it. If we do not want to rely on immigration then it is up to us to ensure that our indigenous workforce – of all ages – is much more fully engaged in the labour market.

The Impact on the Economy

Economists generally agree that as a society ages its rate of economic growth will slow. If the population actually shrinks, it would be logical to expect growth to slow even further. In Britain, the outlook is better than in most other European countries because our working age population should remain broadly stable for the next few decades, even if immigration declines. But the number of over-65s is still going to rise from ten million today to 15 million in 2035.

Yet although the extra burden this will impose will be very significant, surprisingly little thought has been given to the likely impact on the economy. Even now, there is a disturbing tendency to assume that, although health care and pensions will have to rise substantially, this should not have any adverse effect on those who are going to have to foot the bill. Such an approach was looking increasingly irresponsible, even before the credit crunch. With the Government now admitting that that the financial crisis will double the national debt in less than a decade, it is completely unsustainable.[165]

The Treasury's 2008 estimate that ageing will add just 4% of GDP to overall public spending between now and mid-century was highly optimistic even at the time it was published. Somehow, we are going to have to find ways of accommodating the future costs of ageing, without further burdening those of working age. And at the same time we are going to have to make a start on the long, painful process of paying down the huge extra debt that will be incurred in the next few years.

But it is only very recently, as the impact of the credit crunch has become clearer, that politicians of any party have been prepared openly to admit just how worrying the long-term outlook for Britain's public finances really is. Whoever wins the next election will have to start seriously educating the public about the scale of the fiscal problems we face. The retirement age should also be raised more quickly. In Britain, the pension age for women is set to rise from 60-65 between 2010 and 2020, and then to 68 for both sexes in 2048. In the US, despite its comparatively favourable demographics, the pension age for everybody is meant to rise to 67 by 2027. The UK and other European countries should aim to match this.

The problem, though, is philosophical as well as practical. It was the baby boom that underpinned the rise in public spending as a proportion of GDP during the '70s and '80s and made possible the so-called Europe-

165 *The Budget, Building Britain's Future,* 22 April 2009

an social model of an all encompassing publicly funded welfare state. And it was on the back of this philosophy that government across Europe grew fat, our own included. Big government always depended on buoyant demography; now, as the baby boom unwinds, it will have to do likewise, whatever happens with the credit crunch. This is what the European Commission was really saying when it urged its members to prepare for an ageing society by cutting back and running structural budget surpluses.

But while other governments made some effort before 2007 to prepare for the era of worsening dependency ratios that lies ahead, albeit often half-hearted, in this country we were on a decade long fiscal bender. Gordon Brown frequently claimed that the decisions he took, as Chancellor, on tax and spending, were all made with future stability and prosperity firmly in mind. But significantly increasing spending on the old at the expense of the young hardly looks sustainable from a demographic perspective. To have done so just a few years before the baby boomers are due to retire was downright reckless.

Britain's Role in the World

When it comes to our own role on the world stage, population has never been Britain's strong card. In 1800, we did not even feature in the top ten most populous countries. By 1900, at the height of our might, we just made the list at number nine. But even then we were still behind Russia, Germany and France, and had only recently overtaken Italy. In fact, the highest we ever got in the world's population rankings was number eight in 1930. Today, we are the world's 22nd most populous country.[166]

Clearly, power is not just a question of population, and, officially at least, Britain still sees itself as a world power. But if our experience in Iraq has taught us anything, it should be that manpower – or the lack of it – is once again a crucial constituent of military clout. This is particularly so if you want to intervene in countries that have younger and faster growing populations than your own. It is a similar story with the economy. China and India have always been massively more populous than Britain, but that

166 http://www.prb.org/Datafinder/Topic/Bar.aspx?sort=v&order=d&variable=1

did not stop us colonising one and dominating the other in the days when we were dynamic and they were not. Now that both are fully engaged in the world economy, their demography gives them a big competitive edge.

The lesson of recent years is that not only does the power of numbers still count, but its importance is increasing. For a country that is slipping rapidly down the population hierarchy, this can only mean a diminution in our weight and influence around the world. And what goes for this country, of course, goes for Europe as a whole. It is not just the traditional powers such as Britain and France that need to prepare for a changed balance of power in the world, but the continent in general. Any lingering hope that the EU will develop into a global superpower to rival the US can surely be forgotten. As things are at the moment, Europe looks more likely to become a backwater than a powerhouse.

Within Europe, however, the question of Britain's future influence is more complicated.

This country's comparatively resilient demography could mean that our influence closer to home increases, even as it decreases elsewhere. How much we should try to capitalise on this, in our dealings with other, more demographically challenged EU members is a moot point. This growing divergence between very-low-fertility Europe and the rest could become very divisive over the next 25 years. What will happen to the single currency if some ageing countries effectively go bankrupt? Will the other Euro participants have to bail them out, and if so, how? At the moment Europe has neither common tax nor social security systems. Should Brussels therefore expand its authority to encompass such matters?

For Europhiles and the European Commission this may seem like a good argument to expand the EU's authority. Eurosceptics, particularly in Britain, will draw the opposite conclusion, that we would be far better off keeping our distance from potential demographic bankrupts like Italy and Greece.

Final Word

Before finishing what has been, because of the nature of the subject, a rather gloomy consideration of Europe's demographic prospects, we do need to remind ourselves that population change will bring benefits as well as difficulties.

Around the globe people are living longer, more healthily and more happily. They are seeing fewer of their children die. In many previously poor places, especially in Asia and Latin America, rising numbers are spurring economic development. Nor, despite current worries over rising energy and food prices, is that likely to change over the next few decades. Malthusian alarms have been a recurrent feature of economic life for the last 200 years, but the world has yet to run out of food or any other raw material. If high prices force us to search for greener alternatives and treat the world's natural bounty with more respect, then they will have served a useful purpose.

And even here in Europe there are cautious grounds for hope. In this country we tend to be fatalistic about demography. But if we could achieve a stable population, the advantages not just for the economy, but also for the environment, for the sustainability of welfare, health and other social systems, and for fairness between the generations, would be enormous. Nor should this be impossible. In Britain there are clear signs that fertility may at last be beginning to rise from the lows of recent years. In a generation's time it is perfectly conceivable that we may have managed to re-establish a more stable population, but only if we do something about it. We could step off the demographic roller coaster, if we want to.

Appendix:

World Population Projections and Prospects

The countries with the ten highest populations, today and projected in 2050

2009		2050	
Country	Population in millions	Country	Population in millions
China	1346	India	1614
India	1198	China	1417
USA	315	USA	404
Indonesia	230	Pakistan	335
Brazil	194	Nigeria	289
Pakistan	181	Indonesia	288
Bangladesh	162	Bangladesh	222
Nigeria	155	Brazil	219
Russia	141	Ethiopia	174
Japan	127	Dem. Rep. of Congo	148

Source: UN World Population Prospects

Asia

Throughout recorded history, Asia has maintained its position as the world's most populous continent. Over the last half century, it has significantly extended that lead. Asia today has over four times as many people as Africa, and whereas its population was roughly three times as large as Europe's 50 years ago, now it is nearly six times bigger.

This growth will continue for some time yet, but the pace is slowing. By 2030 Asia's population is projected to increase by another 750 million from today's four billion, compared to a rise of 950 million over the last 20 years. By 2035 the continent is expected to reach five billion, but the rate of growth will vary considerably from country to country, and within the larger countries like China and India it will differ from region to region. Combined with increasing life expectancy, the result will be fast growing but also fast ageing populations

As a general rule, numbers are rising most rapidly in the least developed areas, and slowing in the richest countries. There are, however, plenty of exceptions. It is no surprise that fertility fell below replacement level sometime ago in advanced countries, including Japan, South Korea, Taiwan, Singapore and Hong Kong. But it is also below replacement level in less prosperous Thailand, and close to it in Sri Lanka and impoverished Indonesia. Certain countries, most famously China but also Vietnam and North Korea, have artificially held their fertility rates down by means of draconian birth control policies.

All of which means that, compared to other continents where the trends are much more clearly up or down, the demographic outlook for individual Asian countries is extremely mixed. Afghanistan with a TFR of over six children per woman is projected to see its population rise from 24 million in 2005 to 56 million by 2035, and Pakistan, with a TFR of 4.0, is projected to increase from 165 million to 285 million over the same period. But a surprising number of Asian countries will grow comparatively little, and some, most notably China and Japan will see their populations fall over the course of the next 40 years.

China, India and Japan:

		Population in Millions		
	Current TFR	2005	2035	2050
China	1.8	1312	1462	1417
India	2.77	1131	1528	1614
Japan	1.3	127	114	102

China: China currently has the world's largest population at nearly 1,350 million and many in the West still assume that it will continue to rise rapidly for the foreseeable future. In fact, it is set to grow comparatively slowly up to 2035, when it is expected to peak at just over 1,460 million and then start slowly to decline. This can be put down to the famous one-child policy (OCP) to which the Chinese Government remains committed, at least for the time being.

But the OCP is not universal, it is applied mostly in the cities and China's total fertility rate is, in fact, around 1.8 children a woman – a figure that the UN expects to rise to 1.85 over the next two decades. Even so, Chinese officials insist that without the OCP their population would be at least 300 million more than it is today, and worry that the country faces another population boom as the first single-child generation enters reproductive age over the next decade.

However, the government does now accept that the OCP is going to cause problems further down the line. At the moment some 100 million Chinese are 65 or over – 8% of the population. By 2035 this will have almost trebled to 280 million, or 20% of the population. Whereas in France, it took 115 years, from 1865-1980, for the proportion of the population aged over 65 to double from 7 to 14%, in China it will take just 26 years, from 2000-2026.

Because Chinese parents place a huge premium on having a son, the OCP has also led to an alarmingly skewed gender ratio. On average over recent years, 120 boys have been born for every 100 girls. The normal ratio is 107 to 100. The unbalanced structure and rapid ageing of its population pose a huge challenge to China's long-term growth and prosperity. It also poses a social challenge. China has traditionally placed great store by the extended family. But if the one child policy continues for another genera-tion, many of China's children will grow up not only without brothers and sisters, but without uncles, aunts and cousins as well.

A country where welfare in old age has always been provided by children, now faces the prospect that in a generation's time there will not be enough of them. Today's typical Chinese family is often described as consisting of "one mouth, six pockets" – a single "little emperor" doted on by his parents and two sets of grandparents. Thirty years hence there is more likely to be six mouths to feed and one pocket to pick up the bill.

Yet abandoning the OCP would undoubtedly be fraught with danger for a country that is still at risk from overpopulation. The dilemma the country faces was well summed up by the Chinese demographer, Peng Xi-zhe, although whether the Chinese authorities will succeed in effecting the smooth transition to a looser policy that he foresees, must be doubtful:

Unlike many developed countries, ageing in China is coming at a much earlier stage in terms of socio-economic development. It is also occurring over a shorter time span. At present, the government is insufficiently prepared to cope with the problem.

Some advocate relaxing the OCP to slow down the ageing process and create a relatively favourable age structure in the future. However, the potential increase of young people cannot solve the aging problem in the short to medium term, and could lead to a larger population in the long term, thereby worsening the situation.

A new baby boom is feared because over the next 10–15 years there will be a steady increase in the total number of women of reproductive age. There is concern that the single-child cohort born in the early 1980s will soon marry and produce children, and that any relaxation of the current population policy will have a doubling effect on the total population.

Therefore, the general view is that it is better to wait until the 2010s to make any major policy change so that the overall population age structure can adjust smoothly. Many provinces are now modifying family planning regulations to allow more people in certain categories to have two children. A "natural transition" towards a "two children per family" norm will be gradually put in place.

As for the ageing issue, it is an important period from now till the 2020s. If sufficient jobs can be provided for the largest ever working-age population, there will be a one-time "demographic bonus" for development, such as in Japan, Hong Kong and various other east Asian economies. China, therefore, must grasp the opportunity to develop its economy and reform its social welfare system to cope better with the serious ageing problem after the 2020s. Nevertheless, the transfer of some dependency burden from the current generation to the next is inevitable.[167]

---

167 Abbreviated from Xizhe P, "Is it Time to Change China's Population Policy?", *China: An International Journal*, 2004

India and the subcontinent: Sometime around 2030 India's population should overtake that of China, making it the most populous country in the world. But India is not the only large, rapidly expanding country in the subcontinent and nor, in demographic rather than economic terms, is it the fastest growing.

India's population rose by 250% between 1960 and 2005, from 445 million to 1,130 million, whereas Pakistan grew by nearly 350% over the same period – from 48 million to 165 million. By 2035 India is projected to increase by another 35%, taking it to 1,525 million, while Pakistan should grow by almost 75% to 285 million. Bangladesh is another large, rapidly growing country. After increasing from 54 million in 1960 to 153 million in 2005, the UN projects that it will reach around 210 million by 2035. Alone on the subcontinent, Sri Lanka stands out for its comparatively sedate growth. Its current population of 20 million is double that of 50 years ago; by 2035 it is projected to add only another two million people.

Fertility is highest in Pakistan at 4.0 children a woman, with India at 2.8, Bangladesh at 2.4, and Sri Lanka at 2.2. India is expected to grow at a slower pace than its two large neighbours because, as its economic development outpaces them, the fall in its birth rate is gathering pace. In backward states like Bihar the TFR is still as high as six children a woman. But in the main cities, including Delhi, Bombay and Madras, as well as in the more prosperous southern states of Tamil Nadu and Kerala, fertility has already fallen below replacement level and life expectancy has risen.[168]

Due to their comparatively high fertility, ageing is unlikely to be a problem for any of the three big countries. Mushrooming young populations could well fuel instability in Pakistan and Bangladesh. But for India, fast emerging as one of the world's pre-eminent economic powers, its young population should be an advantage for many years to come. In just five years, between 2010 and 2015, India's population aged 15-64 is set to rise by a staggering 72 million.

India will also age far more slowly than most of its competitors. Whereas 20% of Chinese will be over 65 in 2035, in India it will be under 10%. The only cloud on India's demographic horizon at the moment is the rapid spread of Aids. That apart, and provided it can remain politically stable and

---

168 *Population Projections for India and States 2001-2026*, Report of the Technical Group on Population Projections, National Commission on Population, May 2006

economically vibrant (not an easy combination to pull off, admittedly), the country should be on course for a hefty demographic bonus over the next half century.

Japan: Japan has become the bogeyman of Asian demographics. Its fertility has been below replacement level for more than 30 years, and its population is already shrinking. The country had a baby boom after the war, but it did not last for as long as either Europe's or America's. The latest figures for the country's fertility rate show it at under 1.3, the lowest ever. In Tokyo the TFR has fallen to under one child a woman.[169]

The way in which Japan's age-profile is changing as a result of its prolonged low fertility, is startling. The annual number of births declined from around two million in the early 1970s to around one million today. The number of children under 14 fell from 27 million at the beginning of the 1980s to 17 million in 2005. Meanwhile, the population aged 14-65 is expected to decline from 85 million in 2005 to 65 million in 2035 and around 50 million by 2050.

And all the time, the number of pensioners is increasing, from ten million in 1980, to 25 million in 2005 and an expected 37 million in 2035. By 2050 the UN expects Japan's population to have fallen back from 127 million today to 102 million. This would bring it back to the level of the late 1960s, but with five-and-a-half-times as many over-65s. To cap it all, by 2035 life expectancy in Japan, which is already the highest in the world, is projected to reach 86 years.

Apart from working longer, the only medium-term solution now left to Japan is immigration. But in a society which is overwhelmingly ethnically homogenous, this too is extremely problematic. Immigration into Japan is currently some 30,000 a year which by recent standards is high. The UN's projections assume it will rise higher, to an average of 54,000 a year. But even if this happens it will still be a drop in the ocean by European or North American standards. With immigration unlikely to provide relief, and Japanese women so reluctant to have children, it is hard to see what can turn the situation around.

The Asian Tigers: The expression Asian Tigers was coined to describe the rapid economic rise of a group of Far Eastern countries, originally led by Korea and Taiwan, and which later expanded to encompass China and most

169 *The Times*, 24th August 2005

of South East Asia. But while economic growth in all these countries continues to be strong, their demographic outlook has diverged considerably.

Taiwan[170] and South Korea:

		Population in Millions		
	Current TFR	2005	2035	2050
South Korea	1.2	48	48	44
Taiwan	1.1	23	22	19

In Taiwan and South Korea the demographic outlook today is anything
but tigerish. Fertility in both countries has fallen to a miserly 1.2 children
per woman or less, their populations are essentially static and projected
to start falling in around 20 years time. Both countries are also about to
start ageing at an alarming rate. Today about 10% of Taiwanese and South
Koreans are aged 65 or over, which is healthy compared with more than
17% in Western Europe. But by 2035 this will have doubled to over 25%
and by 2050 the percentage of pensioners is expected to reach over 30%,
which will be worse than in Europe.

Thailand, Malaysia, and Indonesia:

		Population in Millions		
	Current TFR	2005	2035	2050
Malaysia	2.2	26	37	40
Indonesia	2.2	219	278	288
Thailand	1.8	66	74	73

Neighbours they may be, but the demographic projections for these three
countries vary to a surprising extent. Malaysia is the richest and Indonesia
the poorest but both have the same TFR of 2.2. Thailand, with a GDP
per capita some 20% less than Malaysia's, has a TFR of just 1.8. Thanks to
its lower fertility, Thailand will age fairly rapidly, but not as fast as South

170 Taiwan statistics from Council for Economic Planning and Development, Taiwan

Korea or Japan. Its proportion of pensioners will double from 8% today to 17% by 2035. By contrast, both Malaysia and Indonesia will continue to have young, rapidly growing populations through to the middle of the century. Malaysia is projected to grow by 40% between 2005 and 2035, from 25 million today to 37 million in 2035. Indonesia, which is by far the biggest of the three, is projected to grow more slowly, by just over 25% to 278 million in 2035. Both Malaysia and Thailand have net immigration, whereas emigration from Indonesia is quite high at around 150,000 a year.

Vietnam and the Philippines:

		Population in Millions		
	Current TFR	2005	2035	2050
Vietnam	2.1	84	108	111
Philippines	3.1	85	131	146

These two countries have very similar sized populations at the moment, but the Philippines' higher fertility means its population is projected rapidly to outpace Vietnam from now on. This will happen despite a very high rate of emigration from the Philippines at about 175,000 a year compared to a surprisingly low UN figure of 40,000 emigrants annually from Vietnam. Also surprising is that both countries have higher population densities than the UK.

The Middle East and North Africa

Iran and the Arab countries of West Asia (including Iraq):

		Population in Millions		
	Current TFR	2005	2035	2050
Iran	1.8	70	92	97
Iraq	4.1	28	53	64
Jordan	3.1	6	9	10
Saudi Arabia	3.2	24	39	44
Syria	3.3	19	32	37
Yemen	5.3	21	43	54

Numbers right across the Middle East are expected not so much to rise, as to rocket between now and 2035. Twenty years ago the total population of the six countries listed above was 99 million, today it is 168 million. Although the rate of growth is beginning to slow, between them they are still projected to add another 100 million by 2035.

Iran and Egypt apart, historically the Middle East has never been a region of large populations but this is now changing. Iraq, which had 16 million people in 1985, is currently over 30 million and projected to be over 50 million by 2035. By then, too, Yemen will be over 40 million and Saudi Arabia just under. Most striking of all, Iran is projected by then to be over 90 million.

Fertility across the Middle East declined substantially in the 1990s, but at around three children per woman remains significantly higher than in the rest of Asia. Nor, with the exception of Iran, is it expected to decline to replacement level until well into the 2030s. Because of this, the populations of the Middle East are not just going to be larger than those of many European countries from now on, but also much younger. In both Yemen and Iraq over 40% of the population are under 14, while the figure for all the other countries except in Iran is over 30%. By contrast, in Europe it is 15%.

North Africa:

		Population in Millions		
	Current TFR	2005	2035	2050
Algeria	2.4	33	46	50
Egypt	2.9	77	116	130
Libya	2.7	6	9	10
Morocco	2.4	30	40	43
Tunisia	1.9	10	12	13
Sudan	4.2	39	65	76

On the southern shores of the Mediterranean, Morocco and Algeria are projected to see population increases between 2005-2035 of 30 and 40% respectively. In Egypt the rise is projected to be 50%, or nearly 40 million extra people.

That would bring Egypt's population to 116 million by 2035, so its historic position as the largest Arab nation seems secure. The fastest rate of increase in North Africa, though, is projected for the Sudan, where the fertility rate is over four children per woman. Its population is projected to rise from 39 million in 2005, to 65 million in 2035, and over 73 million by mid-century.

If the countries of the Middle East and North Africa were more successful, economically, politically and socially, their young populations could be a huge advantage. But in a region which is already unstable and poor, the worry is that these huge surpluses of young people – and especially young men – could all too easily turn to violence and revolution. As it is, emigration from these six countries is currently running at around 200,000 a year in total.

Israel and Palestine:

		Population in Millions		
	Current TFR	2005	2035	2050
Israel	2.8	7	10	11
Palestine	5.1	4	8	10

None of this provides much reassurance for Israel, the region's odd-man-out demographically as well as in terms of religion and politics. At the turn of the millennium Israel had 6.5 million inhabitants of whom 80% were Jews – their numbers boosted by over a million immigrants who arrived in the 1990s, mostly from the old Soviet Union.[171] The other 20% were overwhelmingly Arabs, whose numbers have doubled due to natural increase over the last 20 years. Of the Arab population, roughly 80% are Muslim, 10% Christian and 10% Druze. [172]

Israel's population is predicted to grow to 10 million by 2035. But while the fertility rate for Jewish women is 2.7, for Arab women in Israel it is 4.7. The Israeli Bureau of Statistics projects the Jewish population to grow to 7.2 million by 2030, from 5.3 million today. The

171 Israel and the Palestinian Territories, Country Brief, Population Resource Centre; http://www.prcdc. org/Israel.pdf

172 ibid

Arab population will grow around twice as fast, from 1.4 million today to 2.4 million by the same point, when Arabs will make up some 24% of the total.[173]

Meanwhile the population of the Palestinian territories is around four million today, compared with just over one million when they were first occupied by Israel in 1974. Two factors dominate Palestinian demography. The first is its age structure, which is among the youngest in the world. In 2005 nearly 18% of the population was below the age of 5, and 46% was below 15. The second is that women in Gaza have 5.6 births, on average, while women in the West Bank (including East Jerusalem) have an average of 4.1 children.[174] Both figures are significantly higher than those for neighbouring Arab countries. As a result the Palestinian population is expected to grow from 3.8 million in 2005 to 6.5 million by 2025 and over 8 million by 2035.

Many observers think even this projection from the UN underestimates the likely increase in the Palestinian population. Taking Israel and Palestine as one unit, at the moment Jews still make up a majority of the population – but not for much longer. By mid-century, the combined population of Israel and the Palestinian territories could well be 70% Arab.

Sub-Saharan Africa
Sub-Saharan Africa's population has grown faster than that of any other region over the past 30 years, despite millions of deaths resulting from the Aids pandemic.

Between 1975 and 2005, it more than doubled, rising from 335 to 764 million, and is currently growing at a rate of 2.5% a year. Fertility levels are still over five children per woman and between 2005 and 2035 the UN expects the sub-Saharan population to increase by another 650 million. By 2035 fertility is expected to fall to around three children per woman, but these will still be young countries with a median age of just 23 compared with 18 now. And the high proportion of young people

173 Israel, Central Bureau of Statistics, press release, 25th March 2008; http://www1.cbs.gov.il/reader/newhodaot/tables_template_eng.html?hodaa=200801056

174 *The World Fact Book*, CIA; https://www.cia.gov/library/publications/the-world-factbook/geos/gz.html

means that their populations will continue to grow, even with Aids curbing life expectancy and emigration from the region running at more than 250,000 a year and expected to increase.

On a brighter note, in the longer term life expectancy is expected to increase faster in sub-Saharan Africa over the next 40 years than anywhere else in the world, from 51 today to 66 by 2050. Partly this is because Aids does now seem to be abating (see below), but also because it is so much lower than elsewhere today that the scope for it to increase is commensurately greater. Here are the UN projections for population growth in the larger African countries up to mid-century, together with their current fertility rates:

West and East Africa:

West Africa	Current TFR	Population in Millions		
		2005	2035	2050
Angola	5.8	17	33	42
Congo*	6.1	59	119	147
Ghana	4.3	22	38	45
Mali	5.5	12	22	28
Niger	7.2	13	38	58
Nigeria	5.3	141	243	289
East Africa				
Ethiopia	5.4	75	143	173
Kenya	5.0	36	69	85
Madagascar	4.5	17	34	43
Tanzania	5.6	39	84	109
Uganda	6.4	29	68	91
Zambia	5.9	11	23	29

*Democratic Republic of Congo

Southern Africa: As always, however, there are exceptions – and in this case, very tragic ones. The Aids pandemic in southern Africa will result in populations in some of these countries stagnating over the decades ahead, despite continued high fertility. In the developed world, HIV infection rates have been held to under 1% of the adult population; in some southern African countries they are as high as 25%. These countries have now regressed demographically, back to an era of high birth rates and high death rates, with little growth in population overall.

Southern Africa:

		Population in Millions		
	Current TFR	2005	2035	2050
South Africa	2.6	48	55	57
Lesotho	3.4	2	2	2
Malawi	5.6	13	29	37
Botswana	5.1	2	2	3
Zimbabwe	3.5	12	19	22
Mozambique	5.1	21	37	44
Namibia	3.4	2	3	4

According to the UN, "in 1985-1990, deaths in Southern Africa were concentrated in young children and older adults, and adults aged 20-49 accounted for 20% of all deaths. By 2005-10, a shift had taken place in the distribution of deaths by age, with 51% of all deaths occurring between the ages of 20-49. Such large increases in mortality deplete the cohorts that are in the prime of their working and parental careers, creating the potential for severe shocks to economic and societal structures." Overall the UN reckons that were it not for Aids, its population projection for the 38 African countries significantly affected by the disease (all of which are sub-Saharan) in 2050, would be 129 million higher.

The impact of Aids on individual countries can be enormous. In South Africa nearly 20% of the population are reckoned to be infected. Over the last 45 years, South Africa's population grew from 17 to 47 million. Over the next 40 years it is expected to rise by just 20%, despite a fertility rate that is currently 2.6. In 1990 average life expectancy in South Africa was 61 years. Because of HIV it is 51 today.

Some of South Africa's smaller neighbours have been hit even harder. In Botswana, the death rate per thousand rose from seven a year in 1990 to 15 in 2005, although it is now falling. In South Africa it rose from 8.5 per thousand to 15, and does not yet appear to be falling. However not all the countries in the region are equally afflicted. The outlook for Malawi is a lot more robust than its neighbours, although the country is a lot less developed. Malawi's death rate has actually fallen since 1990 from 16 per thousand to 12 today. With a TFR of over 5, Malawi's population is projected to more than double between 2005 and 2035.

The projected impact of Aids on populations, not just in Africa but around the world is shown in the table below.

Difference in projected populations between the UN medium variant projections v its no-Aids scenario for groups of affected countries

Group of countries	Population difference (thousands)			Percentage difference		
	2010	2015	2050	2010	2015	2050
All 58 affected countries	-39732	-54263	-158156	-0.9	-1.2	-2.8
38 countries in Africa	-29650	-40848	-129487	-3.7	-4.6	-8.1
4 countries in Asia	-6955	-9249	-20435	-0.3	-0.3	-0.7
11 countries in Latin America and the Caribbean	-1223	-1523	-3323	-0.5	-0.6	-1.2

Source: Population Division of the Department of Economic and Social Affairs of the United Nations Secretariat (2009). *World Population Prospects: The 2008 Revision. Highlights.* New York: United Nations.

The New World and the Old Commonwealth

Australia and New Zealand:

		Population in Millions		
	Current TFR	2005	2035	2050
Australia	1.8	20	26	29
New Zealand	2	4	5	5

Both these countries now have fertility rates marginally below replacement level. Nevertheless, both will continue to grow due to immigration, albeit more slowly than in the past. By 2035 Australia's population is projected to increase from 20 million in 2005 to 26 million, and New Zealand's from four to five million. At least by European standards, their dependency ratios should all remain reasonably healthy.

Australia currently takes about 100,000 migrants and refugees a year. Proportionately this is even more than America, which takes about a million a year but has a population 15 times larger. Many of Australia's immigrants now come from Asia, a far cry from the old days of the "white Australia" policy, as do a majority of migrants to New Zealand.[175]

North America:

		Population in Millions		
	Current TFR	2005	2035	2050
USA	2.1	303	380	404
Canada	1.6	32	41	44

Canada. Canada's fertility rate is now down to a European level, at around 1.6 children per woman on the latest figures. Nevertheless it, too, is projected to continue growing, from, 32 million today to 41 million in 2035, again mainly due to immigration which is running at over 200,000 a year. Even immigration, however, will not be enough to protect Canada from an ageing problem, with its population over 65 projected to increase from 13% in 2005 to 24% in 2035.

The United States. Perhaps the biggest surprise of all in world demography at the moment is the buoyant outlook for the US – and not just compared with other developed countries. By 2035 the UN projects that its population will have reached 380 million, an increase of more than a quarter on the 2005 figure of 303 million. By 2050 it is expected to reach over 400 million.

175 Country Profile, Migration Policy Institute, January 2003

Not only are American fertility rates, at roughly replacement level, significantly higher than those in most other developed countries. The US, for reasons partly cultural, partly historic and partly geographic, also has the ability to absorb a far greater number of migrants than any other country. During the last decade, over a million have arrived legally every year – a level last seen before the First World War. Perhaps another 700,000 arrive illegally, mostly across the Mexican border.[176]

This combination of resilient fertility and high immigration means that, while the median age for a European is expected to rise from 40 today to 46 by 2035, in the US the median age is expected to increase from 36 today to just 40 – lower, as we have already seen, than China's will be by that date. Compared with Europe, where the numbers of working age are projected to fall by a quarter by mid century, the contrast is even starker. In the US the number aged 15-64 is projected to rise from 200 million in 2005, to 225 million in 2035, and 245 million by 2050.

Meanwhile the numbers of people of pensionable age will more than double by 2035 from 38 million in 2005 to over 78 million. With its old age dependency ratio set to decline from five workers per pensioner in 2005 to under three in 2035, America will not avoid the pension and healthcare problems that all industrialised nations will experience. And with a comparatively large proportion of the federal budget spent on these items, the effect on the Government's finances could be severe. But by the standards of what is going to happen elsewhere in the industrialised world, America is set to get off lightly.

The increase in the US population will also lead to a marked increase in urbanisation, especially in states that up to now have remained largely rural. Currently, more than half of all Americans live in 10 of its 50 states, most of them along the coasts. Over the next few decades the country's demographic centre of gravity will shift, and not just from the East coast to the West as it has been doing for some time.

More and more people are now moving to a "new sunbelt" consisting of inland states such as Nevada, Arizona, Texas and Tennes-

176 *Unauthorised Migrants: Numbers and Characteristics*, Pew Hispanic Centre, 2005; http://pewhispanic.org/files/reports/46.pdf

see. Nevada increased its population by nearly 20% between 2000 and 2004.[177] We are often reminded that the US, with 5% of the world's population, uses 25% of its energy. Its thirst for space is just as great. One recent statistic is that each American now occupies about 20% more land for housing, schools, shopping, roads and so on, than he or she did 20 years ago.[178]

For those anticipating the decline of the United States, such figures may come as a shock. However, there is a twist in the tail. The US is far less ethnically homogenous than most European countries or Japan, and this is reflected in the fertility rates for the different groups within it. In 1998 the overall American fertility rate was 2.1, with a level of 1.8 for non-Hispanic whites, 1.9 for Asian and Pacific Islanders, 2.1 for American Indians, 2.2 for Blacks, and 2.9 for Hispanics.[179]

Together with high levels of immigration, the high Hispanic fertility rate will ensure a substantial shift in the ethnic balance of the US by mid-century, especially in the South West where Spanish speakers are likely to form a majority in a number of states, perhaps including California. At the moment 35 million people are classified as Hispanics in the US, or 12% of the population. By 2035 that is expected to double to over 70 million – nearly a quarter of the population.[180]

For the Wasps, the White Anglo-Saxon Protestants who have traditionally held the levers of power in America, the outlook is not nearly so buoyant. US whites, dubbed non-Hispanic whites by the Census Bureau, currently make up 75% of the population, but with a fertility level of 1.8 (about the same as North West Europeans) their numbers are expected to decline from 2030 onwards. By 2050 it is reckoned that whites will account for, at most, half the American population.[181]

177 "300 Million and Counting", *The Guardian*, 13th October 2006; http://www.guardian.co.uk/frontpage/story/0,,1921442,00.html

178 ibid

179 "US Has Highest Fertility Rate in Industrialized World", Population Reference Bureau, 16th December 2005

180 Projected Population of the United States, by race and Hispanic origin, US Census Bureau, 2004; http://www.census.gov/ipc/www/usinterimproj/

181 ibid

Latin America:

	TFR	2005	2035	2050
Argentina	2.2	38	48	51
Brazil	1.9	186	220	218
Chile	1.9	16	20	21
Columbia	2.4	43	59	63
Mexico	2.2	105	129	129
Peru	2.6	29	37	40
Venezuela	2.6	27	39	42

Latin America's demographic outlook is broadly comparable with that of the US. Fertility is currently marginally higher at an average 2.25 although expected to decline. Between 2005-2035 population growth is projected to be around 20% in the Caribbean and 25% in Central and South America, even allowing for emigration from the region of roughly one million a year. Life expectancy is expected to increase from around 73 today to 78 by 2035, and the median age from 27 to 37.

Due to this comparatively rapid ageing, Latin America's dependency ratios will soon begin to deteriorate, although to nothing like the extent of the developed world. In Brazil and Mexico, the two giants of the region, the proportion of over-65s is projected to rise from approaching 7% today to a manageable 15% by 2035. But this will not stop the workforce continuing to grow strongly, by a projected 25% between 2005 and 2035. Provided its leaders make no major political or economic mistakes, Latin America, like India, should be able to benefit from a large and prolonged demographic bonus for decades to come.

Europe

Europe began the 20th century with 25% of the world's population, and finished it with 12%. But, as we have seen, up to now this decline has been relative. Despite the horrors and wars of the first half of the last century, the total number of Europeans kept growing, from around 400 million in 1900 to 550 million in 1950, and over 700 million in 2000.[182]

Today, Europe's people are older than any other continent's and its fertility rate, at 1.5 children per woman, is way below replacement level. Across the continent deaths outnumber births. At the same time life expectancy is increasing, so much so that 19 out of the world's 20 oldest countries, in terms of population age, are European.

In Russia, the other European countries of the former Soviet Union and some East European countries, numbers are already in decline (see below), and across Europe as a whole they are at or very close to their peak. By 2035 Europe's overall population is projected to fall from 730 million today to 715 million and then continue on down to around 690 million by 2050.

Thanks mainly to immigration, the total population of the 27 states that make up the EU is projected by the UN to continue to grow from 490 million in 2005 to 504 million in 2035, before falling back to 490 million in 2050. In the EU pensioners already outnumber children, with 16% of the population under 14 compared with 17% who are over 65. By 2035 a quarter of the population is projected to be over 65, and the ratio of pensioners to children will be two to one. Push on another 15 years and the European Commission's statistical office, Eurostat, expects that by 2050 the working age population of the EU will have declined by over 50 million, or nearly 20%, while those of pensionable age will have more than doubled.[183]

Europe also leads the world when it comes to outright depopulation. In most cases this is the result of record low fertility, although in a few countries, such as Russia and the Ukraine increased mortality following the fall of communism has also played a part. Europe's average TFR of 1.5 is barely two-thirds of replacement level, and although the range runs from as low as 1.3 in Poland and the Czech Republic to as high as 1.9 in Britain, Ireland and France, the majority of countries are at the lower end of the scale.

If all this sounds challenging it is, but the impact will be much more uneven than the overall picture might suggest. While the population of every

182 McEvedy C and Jones R, op cit
183 Population Projections 2004-2050, Eurostat press release, 8th April 2005

European country is ageing, by no means all of them are shrinking. Indeed, some (including Britain) will continue to grow, albeit mainly due to immigration, right through to 2035 and even beyond, while others could see their numbers collapse by as much as 30%.

Russia and the former Soviet Union:

		Population in Millions		
	Current TFR	2005	2035	2050
Russia	1.4	143	125	116
Ukraine	1.3	47	39	35
Belarus	1.3	10	8	7

Not only is Russia firmly in the very low fertility category but, amazingly, life expectancy in the former superpower is lower than it was when communism collapsed, especially for men. Combined with its low birth rate, this means that between 2005--2035 Russia's population is expected to fall by 18 million.

In fact it already is falling, having declined from 148 million in 1990 to 143 million in 2005, despite a sizeable influx of ethnic Russians from elsewhere in the former Soviet Union during the 1990s. Immigration into Russia has dropped back from the high levels of the Nineties, and is projected by the UN to average just 50,000 a year from now on, or 1,000 a week. By comparison, if the population continues to drop as projected, the number of Russians will contract at the rate of 10,000 a week to 125 million by 2035 – back to the level of the mid-1960s. In Ukraine and Belarus the outlook is much the same, with both expected to lose around 20% of their populations by 2035. Ukraine has the dubious distinction of being one of the few countries in the world whose population is projected to be lower in 2050 than it was in 1950, on the medium fertility projection.

Many people in these countries blame their demographic woes on the collapse of the Soviet Union. In Russia fertility was at replacement level in the last years of the Soviet Union, but had dropped to just 1.25 ten years later and has since edged up to 1.37. Meanwhile male life expectancy dropped from an already low 64 when the Berlin Wall fell to just 59 in the first half of this decade, although it is edging up again now. By comparison, male life expectancy in Egypt, a third world former client of the USSR, has risen over the same period from 60 to 68. However in the Asian and Muslim countries of the old Soviet Union the outlook is considerably more buoyant: Azerbaijan, Kazakhstan, Kyrgyzstan, Tajikistan, Turkmenistan and Uzbekistan all have higher fertility rates at or above replacement level, and all of them will see their populations grow through to 2035.

When he was president, Vladimir Putin made demography one of his top priorities, not least for strategic reasons. In 2006 he launched an ambitious programme of benefits for women who have more children, aimed at reversing current trends which he described as "the gravest problem facing contemporary Russia", as this report from *The Independent* explains:

> *President Vladimir Putin has pledged cash bonuses to Russian women who give birth to two or more children to reverse what he says is the gravest problem facing contemporary Russia: a declining population. "The most acute problem in modern-day Russia is demography…we have to stimulate the birth of a second child in every family. This is what we need to resolve this problem: first, a lower death rate: second, an efficient migration policy, and third, a higher birth rate."*
>
> *Under Mr Putin's proposals…… women who give birth to a second child will receive a one-off cash bonus of 250,000 roubles (about £5,000). In a country where many scrape by on a monthly wage equivalent to just £160, the bonus is a generous one. Child benefit will also be increased, from the current level of 700 roubles a month to 1,500 roubles for the first child in the family. Women who give birth to a second child can claim a further 3,000 roubles a month and will receive financial help with child care.[184]*

184 *The Independent*, 11th May 2006

Many doubt that such a system of maternity bribes will have much effect, but even if it fails the prognosis is not necessarily all bad for the Russians. Their life expectancy is poorer than the rest of us, and they are shrinking while their Asian neighbours are growing. But with abundant oil, gas and other natural resources, Malthus's theory that a smaller population should mean larger shares for fewer people might yet come true for Russia. And if prosperity can lift their life expectancy and persuade them to have more babies again, their demographic prospects could be rapidly transformed.

Germany, Austria, Switzerland:

		Population in Millions		
	Current TFR	2005	2035	2050
Germany	1.4	82	76	70
Austria	1.4	8	9	8
Switzerland	1.4	7	8	8

Between them, these three countries form the largest and most distinct demographic group in the EU, and the second largest in Europe, after Russia, Ukraine and Belarus. In 2005, 82 million of their combined population of 97 million lived in Germany.

Even when Germany was divided, West Germany had roughly the same population as Britain, France or Italy. Reunited, it is easily the biggest country in the EU and will remain so either until Turkey joins or, if the UN's projections are borne out, its population is overtaken by Britain later this century. In general, good news about German demography is limited. The country's fertility rate of 1.36 children means that it will age rapidly over the next 40 years, with the percentage of people aged 65-plus rising from 19% in 2005 to 31% in 2035, which will include 9% over 80. Over the same period those aged 15-64 are expected to fall from 67% of the population to 57%.

This will reduce the number of working-age people from 55 million today to 43 million over just a quarter of a century, while the over 65s will increase from 16 million today to 23 million. Germany's prolonged low fertility is the main cause of its demographic problems. The TFR fell below replacement level at the end of the 1960s, and was down to 1.5 by 1980 – earlier even than in Japan and Italy. But Germany also has low immigration, at least compared with other large developed countries. Although it currently takes a little over 100,000 immigrants a year, this equates to just 1.3 per thousand of population. The comparable figures are 7.9 for Spain, 5.6 for Italy, 3.3 for the United States, 3.1 for Britain and even 1.6 for France – which has much higher fertility. The extract below, from research by Deutsche Bank, explores some of the problems facing Germany.

> *Estimates put forward by the Institute for Employment Research in-dicate that, at 20%, the potential labour force will shrink more than twice as fast as the overall population from 2010 to 2050 because of the baby-boom effect ... Without migration, the potential labour force would shrink by 18.2 million, or roughly 40%, by 2050.*

> *Even if the fertility rate rises rapidly to the replacement level it will still not be able to stop the trend that began in the 1970s. At best it might be able to slow it down in the longer run. This is partly because of a phenomenon referred to as demographic echo effect. Since relatively few children have been born since the 1970s, there is now a relative paucity of potential mothers. The number of children born in West Germany declined by nearly half between 1965 and 2004, from 1.04 million to 577,000. The medium variant says that the number of women of child-bearing age will fall from nearly 20 million to just over 14 million in 2050.*[185]

The pattern is much the same in Austria and Switzerland. Both have a TFR of 1.4, but due mostly to immigration (currently 30,000 a year in Austria and 20,000 in Switzerland) both should see some population increase until 2035. However, by then both will also see their proportion of pensioners rise to just over 25%.

185 **"The Demographic Challenge"**, Deutsche Bank Research, May 2006

Eastern Europe:

		Population in Millions		
	Current TFR	2005	2035	2050
Poland	1.3	38	35	32
Czech Republic	1.4	10	10	10
Slovakia	1.4	5	5	5
Hungary	1.3	10	9	9
Bulgaria	1.4	8	6	5
Romania	1.3	22	19	17

Together with the former Soviet Union, Eastern Europe has the questionable distinction of leading the world in depopulation and all the signs are that this dispiriting process will continue for the foreseeable future. Hungary was the first; its numbers peaked in 1980, nearly 25 years before Japan's population started to fall. It was followed in the '80s by Bulgaria and Romania, and then in the '90s by the three Baltic States, Latvia, Lithuania and Estonia. Both the Slovak and Polish populations are peaking about now, and Poland may already have started to decline.

All these countries were part of the Soviet bloc and their demography reflects this. In Hungary, population growth stalled for almost a decade following the failed uprising of 1956. In all the others, except Poland and Slovakia, fertility rates dipped in the 1960s, before reviving in the 1970s and 1980s in response to the pro-natalist policies pursued under communism. Even Hungary managed fertility rates of nearly two children per woman right up to 1990, although it was already depopulating. All the others achieved replacement rate or slightly more for as long as the iron curtain remained in place.

But as soon as it was lifted, fertility collapsed. In Latvia, the TFR went from 2.1 to under 1.2 in the space of ten years. Although birth rates across the region have edged up since then, they remain very low with most at 1.4 children per woman or less. In Poland, which with 38 million people accounts for more than half the population of the region, the TFR is 1.27, compared with 2.15 in the last days of communism.

Quite why the collapse of communism had such a dramatic effect on fertility is still unclear. It certainly led to far greater economic insecurity, and many of the old pro-natalist policies and subsidies were quickly scrapped or reduced. It also opened Eastern Europe to Western ideas, including the Western European pattern of fewer children. And when EU accession freed up emigration to the rest of Europe, this fuelled a huge exodus of young, trained people to the West.

Now, it seems likely that some at least of the hundreds of thousands who left may be beginning to return, although reliable figures are hard to come by. In the meantime, the post-communist fertility slump in Eastern Europe has been going on for nearly 20 years with no sign of any meaningful upturn. Even if many of the recent emigrants from the region return, the demographic outlook for these countries over the next half-century will be daunting. Between 2005 and 2035 Bulgaria is projected to lose 25% of its population and Lithuania nearly 20% while Latvia, Hungary and Poland are projected to lose a further 10% each.

Portugal, Spain, Italy and Greece:

		Population in Millions		
	Current TFR	2005	2035	2050
Portugal	1.4	11	11	10
Spain	1.4	43	50	51
Italy	1.4	59	60	55
Greece	1.4	11	11	11

With a TFR of just 1.4 or less, all these countries are relying on immigration to a greater or lesser extent as they try to ward off the sort of dramatic demographic decline that now confronts Germany. All of them also combine very low fertility with high life expectancy. It is this combination that makes their future dependency ratios so scary. By 2035 nearly 30% of Italians will be over 65, and the figure is expected to rise to 33% by 2050 – even allowing for immigration. The projected over-65 figures for Greece and Portugal in 2035 are 26% apiece, and for Spain 25%.

Unsurprisingly, given the speed at which they are ageing, both Italy and Spain have sucked in large numbers of immigrants. Between 2000 and 2005 annual net immigration to Spain averaged 500,000, or 12 migrants per thousand population per annum. In Italy the comparable figures were an annual 350,000, or six migrants per thousand population per annum. Even Portugal and Greece, both traditionally emigrant countries, have recently been taking 40,000 and 30,000 respectively per annum. Italy, in particular, also gets many illegal immigrants, a problem exacerbated by proximity to North Africa. To counter illegal immigration, Spain actively encourages Spanish speaking Latin American migrants in the hope of discouraging arrivals from the Maghreb.[186]

In its 2004 projections the UN had expected Italy's population to fall by nearly 20%, from 59 to 50 million, by 2035. Thanks to immigration, it revised this up to 55 million in its 2006 projections, and in the latest 2008 series that has been revised upwards yet again to 60 million. Likewise the UN had Spain falling from 44 to 42 million by 2035 in its 2004 series. In 2006, given the huge scale of recent immigration into the country, that was revised and the UN instead had Spain growing to 47 million by 2035. In the 2008 series the 2035 projection was revised upwards yet again, to 50 million for 2035.

However, it should be stressed that the UN's figures not only assume that immigration will continue at high levels, but also that fertility in these countries will start recovering quite quickly from now on, to reach at least 1.75 children per woman by 2050. In all four of them, the last time it was at this level was in the 1980s.

The Netherlands, Belgium, Luxembourg, France and Ireland:

		Population in Millions		
	Current TFR	2005	2035	2050
Netherlands	1.7	16	18	17
Belgium	1.8	10	11	11
Luxembourg	1.7	0.5	0.6	0.7
France	1.9	61	67	68
Ireland	2	4	6	6

186 Moreno Fuentes F, "The Regularisation of Undocumented Migrants as a Mechanism for the 'Emerging' of the Spanish Underground Economy", Unidad de Políticas Comparadas, CSIC, 2005

Together with the UK, Western Europe stands out for its comparatively high fertility rates. While elsewhere in Europe the TFR is typically around 1.4, in all these countries it is at least 1.7. In the largest of them, France, it is a near replacement 1.9. What is more, these are UN projections and, as with most developed countries, they are based on the assumption that fertility will converge at 1.85 children per woman. However, this could well turn out to be an underestimate because, in stark contrast to the rest of the continent, fertility in Western Europe is increasing. The Netherlands and Belgium both hit their fertility low points in the early '80s, and France in 1990 when its TFR fell to 1.7. Since then fertility has risen across most of the region, and strongly so in France where the TFR recently hit 2.

In 2006 France produced 830,000 babies whereas Germany, which has a population 20 million bigger, produced just 686,000. Only in Ireland has fertility fallen in recent decades, and that was from its previous very high levels (it had a TFR of 3.5 as late as 1975). It is now steady at around 2.0 – putting it on a par with France.

The other factor that the UN probably underestimates in Western European countries is immigration, as their own national projections often do. After Ireland opened its doors to arrivals from the new Eastern European members of the EU in 2004, its 2006 Census put the population of Eastern Europeans at 145,000 (and rising rapidly) out of a total population 4.2 million.[187] Yet the UN reckons total immigration into Ireland has been running at just 40,000 a year over this period. Meanwhile France has only just begun to accept workers from the countries that joined the EU in 2004, although not from Romania and Bulgaria, which may yet push its arrivals up.

None of this, though, will prevent Western Europe from ageing significantly over the next half century. At the moment over-65s account for 11% of the population in Ireland and 16% in France. By 2035 around 25% of the population is projected to be over 65 in both countries. Once again, though, there is reason to hope that things will turn out better than the UN figures currently predict, given the comparatively high levels of both fertility and immigration in the region.

187 Central Statistics Office Ireland, 2006 Census; http://www.cso.ie/statistics/nationalityagegroup.htm

Scandinavia:

	Current TFR	Population in Millions		
		2005	2035	2050
Denmark	1.8	5	6	6
Finland	1.8	5	5	5
Iceland	2.1	0.3	0.4	0.4
Norway	1.9	5	6	6
Sweden	1.8	9	10	11

Demographic prospects in Scandinavia are very much like those in Western Europe. All of these countries saw immigration rise substantially in the 1990s and the first half of this decade and are now reducing it. In terms of ageing, the proportion of pensioners will rise substantially between now and 2050, but not to more than 25% which is good by European standards.

Turkey:

	Current TFR	Population in Millions		
		2005	2035	2050
Turkey	2.1	71	93	97

If Turkey ever does join the EU, its demography will assume considerable importance for the rest of Europe. The Turkish population is projected to increase strongly, from 71 million in 2005 to 93 million in 2035. This would mean that were it to join the EU sometime around 2020, Turkey would immediately supplant Germany as the biggest member state.

Currently some 6% of its population are aged over 65. By 2035 that will reach 12%, and by 2050 it is projected to hit 18%. But while this will pose a challenge, it will not be anything like as severe as that faced by today's EU countries. Economically, the most significant aspect of Turkey's future demographic growth will be the expected rise of 17 million up to 2035 in the number aged 15-64, which means that it should be well placed to take economic advantage of its rising population whether or not it joins the EU. Just as Europe's demographic window is closing, Turkey's is opening.

Tables

The ten countries or areas with the highest and ten countries or areas with the lowest total fertility rate

2005-2010		
Rank	Country	Total Fertility Rate
	A. Highest fertility	
1	Niger	7.15
2	Afghanistan	6.63
3	Timor-Leste	6.53
4	Somalia	6.40
5	Uganda	6.38
6	Chad	6.20
7	Dem. Republic of the Congo	6.07
8	Burkina Faso	5.94
9	Zambia	5.87
10	Angola	5.79
	B. Lowest fertility	
1	China, Macao SAR	0.95
2	China, Hong Kong SAR	1.02
3	Bosnia and Herzegovina	1.21
4	Republic of Korea	1.22
5	Malta	1.26
6	Japan	1.27
7	Poland	1.27
8	Singapore	1.27
9	Slovakia	1.28
10	Belarus	1.28
	WORLD	2.56

Source: Population Division of the Department of Economic and Social Affairs of the United Nations Secretariat (2009). *World Population Prospects: The 2008 Revision. Highlights.* New York: United Nations.

Note: Only countries or areas with 100,000 persons or more in 2009 are considered.

The ten countries with the youngest and ten with the oldest populations

	2009	
Rank	Country or area	Median age
	A. Oldest population	
1	Japan	44.4
2	Germany	43.9
3	Italy	43.0
4	Finland	41.8
5	Channel Islands	41.7
6	Switzerland	41.6
7	Bulgaria	41.5
8	Austria	41.4
9	Slovenia	41.4
10	China, Hong Kong SAR	41.3
	B. Youngest population	
1	Niger	15.1
2	Uganda	15.5
3	Dem. Republic of the Congo	16.5
4	Burkina Faso	16.7
5	Zambia	16.8
6	Malawi	16.8
7	Afghanistan	16.8
8	Chad	17.0
9	Timor-Leste	17.2
10	Angola	17.3
	WORLD	28.9

Source: Population Division of the Department of Economic and Social Affairs of the United Nations Secretariat (2009). *World Population Prospects: The 2008 Revision. Highlights.* New York: United Nations.

Note: Only countries or areas with 100,000 persons or more in 2009 are considered.

Countries or areas whose population is projected to decrease between 2009 and 2050

Rank	Country or area	Population (thousands) 2009	2050	Difference Absolute	Percentage
1	Bulgaria	7 545	5 392	-2 153	-28.5
2	Belarus	9 634	7 275	-2 359	-24.5
3	Republic of Moldova	3 604	2 734	-870	-24.1
4	Ukraine	45 708	35 026	-10 682	-23.4
5	Lithuania	3 287	2 579	-708	-21.5
6	Bosnia and Herzegovina	3 767	3 008	-758	-20.1
7	Japan	127	101 659	-25 498	-20.1
7	Romania	21 275	17 279	-3 996	-18.8
8	Russian Federation	140	116 097	-24 777	-17.6
9	Latvia	2 249	1 854	-395	-17.6
10	Poland	38 074	32 013	-6 060	-15.9
11	Germany	82 167	70 504	-11 663	-14.2
12	Croatia	4 416	3 825	-591	-13.4
13	Hungary	9 993	8 934	-1 059	-10.6
14	TFYR Macedonia	2 042	1 857	-186	-9.1
15	Slovakia	5 406	4 917	-489	-9.0
16	Estonia	1 340	1 233	-107	-8.0
17	Serbia	9 850	9 193	-657	-6.7
18	Portugal	10 707	10 015	-692	-6.5
19	Italy	59 870	57 066	-2 804	-4.7
20	Channel Islands	150	144	-6	-4.0
21	Slovenia	2 020	1 954	-66	-3.3
22	Greece	11 161	10 939	-222	-2.0
23	Montenegro	624	618	-6	-0.9
24	Czech Republic	10 369	10 294	-75	-0.7

Source: Population Division of the Department of Economic and Social Affairs of the United Nations Secretariat (2009). *World Population Prospects: The 2008 Revision. Highlights.* New York: United Nations.

Note: Refers only to countries or areas with 100,000 persons or more in 2009.

Average number of live births per year (1000s)

	1960-65	1965-70	1970-75	1975-80	1980-85	1985-90	1990-95	1995-00	2000-05
World	111 829	117 740	119 550	120 479	128 653	136 825	135 888	133 632	133 493
Europe (1)	11 873	10 838	10 453	10 128	10 080	9 806	8 366	7 431	7 419
Africa	14 449	16 066	18 151	20 550	23 311	25 728	27 850	30 062	32 816
Asia	70 704	76 143	75 917	74 190	78 945	84 627	82 844	79 547	76 623
Latin America and the Caribbean	9 691	10 233	10 804	11 389	11 769	11 790	11 757	11 683	11 601
Northern America	4 663	4 002	3 735	3 760	4 064	4 356	4 518	4 341	4 461
Oceania	449	459	491	463	484	518	554	567	573
EU-27	7 595	7 501	6 944	6 473	6 166	5 919	5 554	5 106	5 059
China	26 313	28 798	25 131	20 745	21 627	24 721	21 555	19 848	17 569
India	19 108	20 241	21 699	23 452	25 048	26 524	27 890	27 728	27 408
Japan	1 662	1 793	2 147	1 759	1 533	1 281	1 213	1 213	1 141
Russian Federation	2 585	1 854	2 027	2 163	2 371	2 363	1 620	1 326	1 441
United States	4 197	3 618	3 383	3 396	3 689	3 973	4 123	3 992	4 124

(1) EU-27, Albania, Andorra, Belarus, Bosnia and Herzgovina, Croatia, Faeroe Islands, Iceland, Liechtenstein, the former Yugoslav Republic of Macedonia, Republic of Moldova, Montenegro, Norway, the Russian Federation, Serbia, Switzerland and the Ukraine.

Source: Eurostat (tps00111), United Nations, Population Division of the Department of Economic and Social Affairs.

Total Fertility Rates (average number of children per woman)

	1960-65	1965-70	1970-75	1975-80	1980-85	1985-90	1990-95	1995-00	2000-05
World	4.98	4.90	4.47	3.92	3.58	3.38	3.05	2.80	2.65
Europe (1)	2.58	2.36	2.16	1.97	1.89	1.83	1.57	1.40	1.41
Africa	6.87	6.80	6.72	6.61	6.45	6.13	5.68	5.28	4.98
Asia	5.65	5.67	5.04	4.19	3.67	3.40	2.97	2.67	2.47
Latin America and the Caribbean	5.97	5.54	5.04	4.48	3.92	3.41	3.03	2.73	2.52
North America	3.35	2.55	2.01	1.78	1.81	1.89	1.99	1.95	1.99
Oceania	3.98	3.57	3.23	2.73	2.59	2.51	2.48	2.42	2.37
EU-25	2.64	2.54	2.23	1.94	1.79	1.67	1.56	1.43	1.48
China	5.72	6.06	4.86	3.32	2.55	2.46	1.92	1.78	1.70
India	5.82	5.61	5.26	4.89	4.50	4.15	3.86	3.46	3.11
Japan	2.02	2.00	2.07	1.81	1.76	1.66	1.49	1.39	1.29
Russian Federation	2.55	2.02	2.03	1.94	2.04	2.12	1.55	1.25	1.30
United States	3.31	2.55	2.02	1.79	1.83	1.92	2.03	1.99	2.04

(1) EU-27, Albania, Andorra, Belarus, Bosnia and Herzgovina, Croatia, Faeroe Islands, Iceland, Liechtenstein, the former Yugoslav Republic of Macedonia, Republic of Moldova, Montenegro, Norway, the Russian Federation, Serbia, Switzerland and the Ukraine.

Source: Eurostat (demo_find), United Nations, Population Division of the Department of Economic and Social Affairs.

Speed of Population Aging in Selected Countries

Number of Years for Percent of Population Age 65 or Older to Rise from 7% to 14%

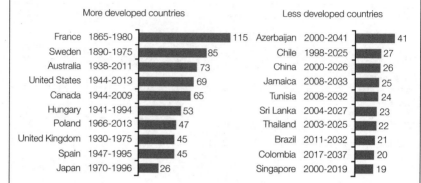

More developed countries				Less developed countries		
France	1865-1980	115	Azerbaijan	2000-2041	41
Sweden	1890-1975	85	Chile	1998-2025	27
Australia	1938-2011	73	China	2000-2026	26
United States	1944-2013	69	Jamaica	2008-2033	25
Canada	1944-2009	65	Tunisia	2008-2032	24
Hungary	1941-1994	53	Sri Lanka	2004-2027	23
Poland	1966-2013	47	Thailand	2003-2025	22
United Kingdom	1930-1975	45	Brazil	2011-2032	21
Spain	1947-1995	45	Colombia	2017-2037	20
Japan	1970-1996	26	Singapore	2000-2019	19

Dates show the span of years when percent of population age 65 or older rose (or is projected to rise) from 7 percent to 14 percent.

Source: K. Kinsella and Y.J. Gist, *Older Workers, Retirement, and Pensions: A Comparative International Chartbook* (1995) and K. Kinsella and D. Phillips, "The Challenge of Global Aging," *Population Bulletin* 60, no. 1 (2005).

Ratio of the inactive elderly population aged 65 or over to the labour force

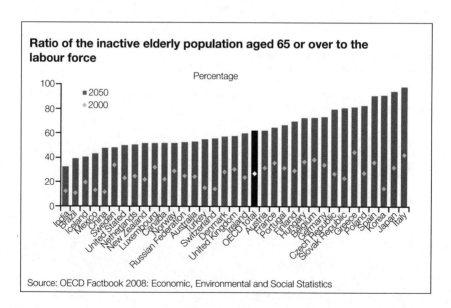

Source: OECD Factbook 2008: Economic, Environmental and Social Statistics